1/03. pg 111 has paper stuck on
lower corners

96	97	98	99	00	03

CATS

The Rise of the Cat

Above *In Pyrenean villages, where cats are expected to earn their living by keeping down the rodent population, cat holes are often cut in house doors.*
Overleaf *The spread of cats around the world has often been aided by man. In Europe the movement of the ginger cat was probably helped by Viking ships.*

CATS

The Rise of the Cat

Roger Tabor

BBC Books

Published by BBC Books,
a division of BBC Enterprises Limited,
Woodlands, 80 Wood Lane, London W12 0TT

First published 1991
Reprinted 1991, 1992
© Roger Tabor 1991

The moral right of the author has been asserted

ISBN 0 563 36011 9

Designed by Tim Higgins

Artwork on p. 96 drawn by Angela McAllister

Set in Esprit by Ace Filmsetting Ltd, Frome, Somerset
Printed and bound in Great Britain by Clays Ltd,
St Ives plc
Colour separations by Technik Ltd, Berkhamsted
Jacket printed by Belmont Press Ltd, Northampton

Author's Acknowledgements

It is impossible to list all the people and organisations
involved during the eight years that this project has
been in preparation. For bringing the TV series into
existence I must thank Dick Meadows, Sally Wilson,
Alan Neale, Paul Fitzgerald, Linda Hutchings,
Stephanie Crowther, Fred Sturman, John Marshall-
Potter, Romany Helmy, Wiyada Tasakorn and Naeko
Funakoshi; and for their hard work behind the book Liz
Artindale, Pat Simonet, Sheila Ableman, Martha Caute,
Jennifer Fry, Esther Jagger and Tim Higgins.

Thanks are also due to the British Museum (Natural
History); the British Museum Egyptology Dept; Cairo
Museum, Dept of Antiquities, Egypt; National Museum
of Thailand; Chelmsford Museum, Colchester Museum,
Office National de la Chasse; Cat Survival Trust; the
organisers of the National Cat Show; Essex Cat Show;
TICA (New York and Los Angeles); Venice DINGO;
the Pet Food Manufacturers' Association; Zagazig
University; Boca Raton Humane Society; Wat Phailom,
Dawn and Gotoku-ji Temples; Alain Zivie; Juliet
Clutton-Brock; Roy Robinson; Jerry Heath; Bilâl
Gündüz; Masako Takeuchi; Keith Hopkin; Bernice
Mead; Ros Elliott; Wendy Thornton; Barbara Castle;
Jean Murchison; Viki Markstein; Ed and Malee Rose;
Kutbettin Bahadir; Nick Wickenden; Peter Minter;
Peter Churcher; Peter Borchelt; Paul Casey; Carol
Pedley; Ann Baker; Gay Frank; Hank and D. D. Tyler;
Brian Fitzgerald; Prof. M. Bakr; Anusorn Sapmanu;
Bess Higuchi and Ikram Kali.

The translation of 'Messe ocus Pangur Ban' from the
Codex Sancti Pauli is by Robin Flower.

Picture Credits

Nigel Adams 87; Aga-Rayburn 187; Animal
Photography 109 (Sally Anne Thompson); Ardea 78
(John Daniels), 81, 94-5 (J.-P. Ferrero), 170 (J. M.
Labat); Liz Artindale/Tabor Picture Library 102, 139,
154, 158, 162; Barnaby's Picture Library 70-1 (Tony
Boxall), 74 (Elizabeth Goodwin), 79 (Mustograph), 123
(W. Lüthy), 178-9 (M. Campbell-Cole); Belgian Tourist
Office 42; Bridgeman Art Library 114; British Library
31 (MS Harl. 6563, f.40); British Museum 21, 33, 104,
146; Jean-Loup Charmet 44-5 below; Bruce Coleman
2-3 (Jane Burton), 45 top (Kim Taylor), 46 (Kim
Taylor), 47 (Hans Reinhard), 48 (Kim Taylor), 54
(Jane Burton), 75 top (Hans Reinhard), 84 (Jane
Burton), 103 (Hans Reinhard), 106 (Hans Reinhard),
128 (Hans Reinhard), 150 (Fritz Prenzel), 155 (Jane
Burton), 156 (Jane Burton); Dean and Chapter of
Winchester 50 (Warburg Institute); ET Archive 175;
Mary Evans Picture Library 41, 124; Fotomas 59; Sally
and Richard Greenhill 182; Robert Harding Picture
Library 157, 166; Hulton-Deutsch Collection 56;
Images Colour Library 44 top; Metropolitan Museum of
Art, NY 8-9, 18-19 (both Egyptian Expedition, Rogers
Fund, 1930), 142-3 (Fletcher Fund, 1947); Musée
d'Aquitaine, Bordeaux 30 (J. M. Arnaud); National
Gallery, London 115; Alan Neale 1; NHPA 91 (G. B.
Baket/ANT); Prince Sadruddin Aga Khan Collection
117; Scala 6-7, 35, 101; Scott Polar Research Institute
86; Frank Spooner/Gamma 158-9; Roger Tabor 13, 14,
15, 22, 23, 24, 27, 28, 37, 38, 53, 62-3, 64, 66-7, 69, 73,
75 below, 83, 92, 98, 112-13, 118-19, 120-1, 126, 127,
130, 134, 135, 138, 144, 147, 160, 164, 167, 168, 171,
173, 177, 183, 186, 188, 189; University College,
London (Petrie Museum, Dept of Egyptology) 11.

Contents

Pliny wrote of cats: 'With what silent stealthiness, with what light steps do they creep towards a bird!' In Roman Britain cats lived in villas as pets of the aristocracy, as depicted in this mosaic of a mackerel tabby.

The Cult of the Cat

The Egyptians believed that at night the sun's rays were held in the cat's eyes, to which they attributed their reflective quality. Here the sun god Ra in the form of a cat raises a knife to sever the head of the serpent Apop, god of darkness and chaos. Wall painting, c.1300 BC, from a tomb at Deir el Medina.

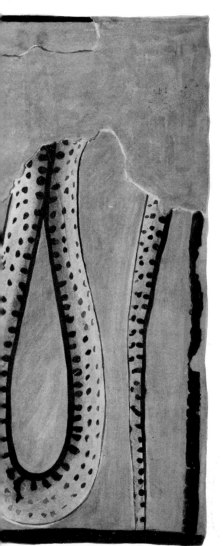

1 Ancient Deities

The cat is like no other animal. People are rarely neutral about cats, and fortunately today more people love them than hate them. In its time the cat has been seen as both demon and divinity, and yet most are now pets. One of the newer stars on the cat stage is the Egyptian Mau, which I went to see amid all the razzmatazz of New York's Madison Square Garden cat show. It was the USA that first gave the breed official recognition, as recently as 1968; that was ironic, for the Mau was taken from the streets of Egypt and is a direct descendant of the first domestic cat thousands of years ago.

At first, the cat was revered as a god. The lion and the cat were among a number of creatures sacred to the Ancient Egyptians, and cats were venerated as a national deity for more than 1300 years. When the cult was at its height, in the fifth century BC, the Persian army under King Cambyses attacked Egypt. Exploiting the enemy's weakness, the invaders attached cats to their shields in the certain knowledge that the Egyptians would be unable to inflict injury on them. It was a strategy that worked spectacularly, for Cambyses conquered Egypt and started a new dynasty of pharaohs.

So revered were cats that, as the Sicilian Diodorus

recorded while visiting Egypt during the Roman occupation in the first century BC, rough justice could be meted out to those who ill-treated them – a soldier who drove his chariot over a cat in Alexandria was stoned to death by the enraged mob. Other foreign eye witnesses reported the rituals associated with a house cat's death: its owners would go into mourning and shave off their eyebrows.

The cat goddess

The feline divinity that inspired such devotion was the fertility goddess Bastet, who was first worshipped in the form of a lioness. From the earliest times the Egyptians saw a link between the searing heat of the desert and the ferocious strength of the lion. The lion-bodied Sphinx was a symbol of the sun gods Ra and Horus, facing east to meet the sun as it rose each day across the Nile. Ra's aggressive eye gave forth arid heat from the lioness-headed Sakhmet, while the productive warmth of Ra's gentle eye came from Bastet.

At all periods during the worship of Bastet she could be lioness-headed, but with the emergence of the domestic cat she began to be portrayed in bronzes and carvings as either a cat or a cat-headed woman. Bastet was a goddess with lunar as well as solar aspects. To the Egyptians, the reflective eye which characterises the cat at night held the sun's rays while it was out of sight; and each night, as an aspect of the god Ra, the cat fought the terrible serpent of darkness, Apop.

The cat and the scarab

The scarab or dung beetle was also sacred to the Ancient Egyptians. In the beetle's continual task of rolling large balls of life-giving dung, which enabled the crops to grow, they saw an image of the god Ra rolling the ball of the sun across the sky each day. Bronzes of Bastet frequently have scarabs on their foreheads, emphasising their link with Ra; I believe the Egyptians saw the pattern of a scarab in the tabby markings on the cat's forehead.

A pyramid for cats

The famous pyramids at Giza were sun symbol tombs for the pharaohs, built to face Ra directly at sunrise and sunset. Abydos is one of the oldest necropolises in Egypt; in 1921–2, when it was excavated by the famous archaeologist Sir Flinders Petrie, a small pyramid was found for

At Abydos a pyramid for cats was discovered in the 1920s. They were buried with gifts for the afterlife, which suggests that they were temple cats considered to be incarnations of Bastet.

that sun symbol the cat. The central chamber contained skeletons of seventeen cats. In front of them was a row of offering pots that are believed to have contained milk for the afterlife of these animals – a direct echo of the burial goods left in the tombs of the pharaohs for their continued existence as gods. Such an extraordinary entombment suggests that these cats were probably kept at a temple as incarnations of the Bastet deity.

Bubastis

The centre of cat worship was Bastet's temple at the ancient city of Bubastis in the Nile delta. Built on an island formed by two artificial channels that connected to the Nile, it housed these special cats whose needs were attended to by the young women of the temple. The earliest part of the building, erected by the 4th Dynasty pharaohs Cheops and Chephren (2550–2490 BC), who also built the Sphinx to front their pyramids, was dedicated to Bastet as the lioness of the sun; later parts were devoted to the small cat. Elsewhere in Egypt other lion-headed deities were also local gods, such as Pakhet at Beni Hassan and Sakhmet at Memphis. But it was at Bubastis that the cat turned from a local goddess into a national deity.

Libyan chieftains had settled in the delta, and one of them, Seshonq, seized the throne of Egypt, founding the 22nd Dynasty (945–712 BC). He made Bubastis the new capital, and Bastet was given precedence over other goddesses. Today her granite temple is in ruins, yet at the height of its activities, when it was visited by the Greek historian Herodotus in the fifth century BC, he stated that 'there is none so pleasant to the eye as this [temple] of Bubastis'. The annual festival of Bastet was the largest of

An Ancient Egyptian cat-headed bronze of the goddess Bastet, holding the traditional sistrum and with the customary four kittens at her feet.

such occasions in all Egypt, with over 700,000 devotees flocking there during April and May.

The crowds arrived in boatloads; the women shook rattles known as sistra and flutes were played, accompanied by singing and clapping. As the craft sailed past villages and towns the women called out in a provocative way to those on the bank, often lifting their clothes right over their heads. During the no doubt wild celebrations, Herodotus wrote, more wine was drunk than during the whole of the rest of the year.

The bronzes of Bastet in cat-headed form carry the sistrum, the aegis shield and a basket, a strange collection of items which probably reflects the appearance of the devotees. The sistrum portrayed with the fertility goddesses Bastet and Hathor was a percussion instrument which sounded the rhythm of lovemaking. The Greek author Plutarch, who observed these rituals during the first century AD, wrote that the roundness of the sistrum represented the lunar sphere, above which was the moon's representative, the cat. The side arms on the sistrum symbolised the horns of Hathor, whose emblem was a cow.

Plutarch also recorded that the cat had a physical link with the moon, for the pupil of its eye grew larger or smaller depending on whether the moon was waxing or waning. The moon was also connected with women, through their monthly cycle; and so the moon, women and cats were seen to be interconnected. The female cat usually gives birth to four kittens, a fact recognised by the Egyptians, for the cat-headed bronzes of Bastet normally have four kittens at her feet; and there were four moving bars in the sistrum.

THE CULT OF THE CAT

Sacred cats

Although there were special temple cats the cult extended to household cats, as Herodotus recorded: 'Cats on their decease are taken to the city of Bubastis, where they are embalmed, after which they are buried in sacred repositories.' Amid the hustle and bustle of big festivals the purpose-wrapped mummies of cats reared at the temple were sold to devotees. It must have been a lucrative trade, with demand exceeding supply, for in some instances fraudulent mummies were peddled.

In 1981 the historical zoologist Juliet Clutton-Brock found by X-raying mummies that some of them had broken necks, which she believes was the cause of their death. At first sight this appears to contradict the Ancient Egyptian reverence for the cat, but most religions contain

The probable forebears of the domestic cat: Felis lybica, *the African wild cat* (left), *which has both spotted and striped varieties, and* Felis chaus, *the jungle or marsh cat* (opposite).

an element of ritual sacrifice of the deity. At the cat temple or Bubastion in Saqqara there were many kitten mummies, and it seems probable that kittens were taken to the shrine by female devotees in baskets of the form carried by Bastet. However, many mummified cats had reached a good age.

But were cats only mummified? Edouard Naville, the nineteenth-century excavator of Bubastis, believed that more cats were ritually cremated than mummified, and at both Saqqara's Bubastion and the cat temple of Pakhet at Beni Hassan there is evidence of extensive use of fire in the past. If cremation of cats took place, too, then the number 'processed' becomes even more incredible than the enormous volume mummified.

So when did man first start his relationship with the cat, and when did domestication occur?

THE CULT OF THE CAT

From wild to domestic

The origin of the domestic cat has lain shrouded in mystery for centuries. Its likely forebears come from the twenty-five species of true small wild cats that are found around the world. Many will interbreed and hybridise, and consequently a number of them have been suggested as forming part of the ancestry of today's cat; they include the golden cat, the leopard cat, Pallas's cat and the sand cat. The main contender is the African wild cat (*Felis lybica*), which is a southern form of the forest wild cat (*Felis silvestris*) found in Britain and mainland Europe. However the Ancient Egyptians mummified the jungle or marsh cat (*Felis chaus*) as well as the African wild cat, yet its input has largely been ignored.

While the European/African wild cats have stripes and spots on their coats, the jungle cat is more like an Abyssinian in not having markings on its body. Although these are all true wild cats, if the European or African wild cat mates with a domestic cat the kittens usually retain the wildness and are little balls of fire, whereas those from a jungle cat/domestic cat mating will be more humanisable. This feature of the jungle cat could have been useful in the initial period of domestication with the African wild cat.

Although there are a few remains of cats in other countries, none give any solid evidence of domestication outside Egypt.

Tomb paintings

Egyptian tomb paintings are the best guide to when the cat became domesticated. There are two types: those with cats in marshland settings hunting for birds, and those where the cat is in a more obvious domestic setting underneath its lady owner's chair.

Among the earliest, from around 2000 BC, is in the tomb of Khnumhotep at Beni Hassan; it is a true wild animal, a superbly accurate painting of the marsh cat. The tomb is close to the Pakhet cat temple which was later shaped to its present form by Queen Hatshepsut, so the painter's familiarity with this elusive animal was probably due to wild cats being kept at the temple site. A second group of marsh hunting scenes includes the famous 18th Dynasty painting of Nebamun fowling in the marshes, which is described below. The time when these scenes were painted overlaps with the appearance of images of cats beneath the chairs of their women owners. This period's hunting and domestic scenes, dating from between 1475 and 1364 BC, are mainly found in tombs in the Valley of the Nobles at Thebes, and show cats with tabby patterns.

Among the tombs of these noblemen is that of the harbourmaster May; here the cat is shown on a leash in what is probably the earliest clear domestic setting. In the tomb of the priest Nakht the cat is feeding on a fish. By the reign of Amenhotep III (1402-1364 BC) the cat had become part of court life, for one is seen playing with a bird under the seat of the wife of the pharaoh's chief steward. And on the back of the pharaoh's daughter's chair a cat is portrayed underneath a throne on which Queen Tiyi is sitting. The cat could not have been given greater acceptance.

A century later the inhabitants of Deir el Medina, or the town of the workmen - it was a kind of artists' and artisans' colony, housing the families of the men who toiled on the tombs in the Valleys of the Kings and Queens - were painting images of cats on one of their

In this wall painting, c.1275 BC, from a tomb at Deir el Medina, Ipy and his wife receive offerings from their children. A kitten is playing with Ipy's sleeve while an adult cat sits under his wife's chair: in Ancient Egyptian art the image of a cat sitting under a woman's chair was a symbol of fertility.

own tombs, that of a man named Ipy. Not only does the cat sit under the chair of Ipy's wife, but on the arm of Ipy's chair is a kitten playing with his sleeve.

What all the tomb paintings point to is that domestication of the cat probably occurred at the beginning of the 18th Dynasty, around 1500 BC, just three and a half thousand years ago.

Reinterpreting the tomb paintings

The unlikely event of a cat tamely catching ducks in hunting scenes has, amazingly, passed without comment by observers. But in the hunting party portrayed in the painting of Nebamun no cat would act as a retriever after domestication, let alone before. If wild cats were put on leashes to catch prey, they would fight the noose and leash - and trailing a leash noisily would scare away the wildfowl. The Egyptians, who depicted details with great accuracy, would have shown collars and leashes if they had been worn. So what is happening?

These pictures have always been regarded as life scenes because they seem so naturalistic; but this view, I think, is wrong. There is a much more plausible interpretation: we should view the scenes, including the cat's role, as allegorical. Nebamun's hunting party is not a group of huntsmen, but his formally attired family. It is a scene of pleasure, as its accompanying text says: 'having pleasure, seeing good things, trapping birds as a work of Sekhet [the marsh goddess]'. The cat's catch is spectacular, and the man's too as he effortlessly pulls three long-necked birds out of the marsh with one hand. It is hardly accurate - rather it is a reference to the abundance of game.

The Ancient Egyptian concepts of birth and rebirth

Nebamun fowling in the marshes accompanied by a 'retriever' cat, a wall painting from a tomb at Thebes. No cat could be used effectively in such a way; it makes better sense to interpret this painting as an allegory of fertility and plenty.

after death made sexuality important to them. The Egyptologists John Baines and Jaromir Malek have described this painting as covertly erotic, ensuring 'rebirth through potency in the next life' and enabling 'the deceased to lead an enjoyable existence'. Nebamun's wife is unsuitably dressed for such an expedition in a heavy wig. But this is an erotic signal, as shown in a New Kingdom (1567-1085 BC) story of seduction: 'Come, let us spend an hour lying. Put on your wig.' She holds the counterpoise and sistrum, symbolic of sexual goddesses. In this scene, laden with sexual implication, a cat behaving unconvincingly makes more sense when seen allegorically. Showing the cat among other sexual symbols is most appropriate, as Bastet was the goddess of fertility and pleasure.

The cat is also allegorical even in the 'domestic' paintings. Cats always sit under the wife's chair, enhancing her fertility by association with Bastet. Viewing all these images allegorically eliminates the idea of a hunting 'halfway house' of domestication – however implausible that may seem.

Cat coffins

Evidence of the acceptance of the domesticated cat across all levels of society as a household animal is provided by some Egyptian cat coffins. From the reign of Akhenaten, husband of the beautiful Nefertiti, a royal cat on its limestone sarcophagus is portrayed before an offering table in the afterlife, as if she had been a person of noble birth. The embalmed cat mummy once sat inside in a gilded wooden mummy case; the accompanying text calls her 'Lady Cat' and she belonged to Prince Tutmosis, the pharaoh's brother. But personal coffins were not just for royalty, as is demonstrated by a small clay coffin, still containing the remains of a young cat, from the workmen's town of Deir el Medina.

How did domestication happen?

The domestic cat is unique in that it became a species at the time of the development of towns. Dogs and cattle had much earlier links with mankind, from the period when hunting and farming developed. Was the rise of the town instrumental in the domestic cat's origin, or merely coincidental? But deified cats were kept in temples and, like the pharaohs, preserved after death. So could penning together species of wild cats in temples have resulted in domestication? The crucial question is: did the domestic cat have a town origin or a temple origin?

A royal burial: the limestone sarcophagus of the cat that belonged to Prince Tutmosis (opposite) *shows a cat with an offering table, portrayed as if it were a noble human being. Elaborate linen wrappings* (below) *were reserved for special cats or those of noble owners.*

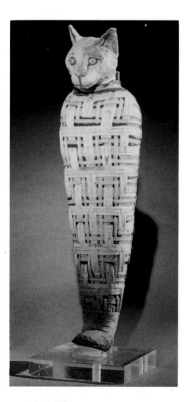

The town theory

From the ruins of Deir el Medina it is possible to see how its inhabitants lived. This community of craftsmen left a superb record of their way of life, from which we know that cats formed part of it. The town consisted of around 120 houses, with a narrow main street and some side alleys running off it, just like the old bazaar in Cairo today. The buildings had yards with kitchens at the back. Those African wild cats sufficiently tolerant of man hunted around town after easy prey, such as the rodents and birds associated with human settlements. The most confident of the cats lived from scavenging waste food from the yards and small streets and over time a sizeable population would have built up, breeding within itself. The town became a local island supporting a high density of cats; as a result far more bred in that small area in any generation than could have done so over thousands of square miles of desert or over many generations. Towns provided a selection pressure which gradually changed the animal, accelerated by the larger population of cats.

In Cairo today, and around the cities and islands of the Mediterranean, feral cats are found readily scavenging, reliving the possible birth of a new species: the domestic cat. Cats sit hopefully at today's tavernas looking at tourists, just as their ancestors did at the feet of the street vendors and eating house customers of Ancient Egypt.

The temple theory

An alternative route to domestication may have occurred as, over hundreds of years, the African wild cat and the jungle cat were enclosed together on temple sites, probably producing a hybrid. However until recently the evidence has been only fragmentary. Cat cemeteries had been found for a long time, but plundered. In the days of Napoleon a French military administration set fire to one in order to discover its size: it was still burning a week later. During the second half of the nineteenth century many Egyptian bronze cats and occasionally cat mummies found their way on to the European museum and collectors' market. But since most had been dug and sold illicitly, it was not usually possible to attribute them to particular sites. And then a huge find of cat mummies was made at the site of an ancient temple dedicated to the cat goddess of the Middle Nile, Pakhet.

In 1889 the steamer *Pharos and Thebes* docked at Liverpool with a consignment of 19½ tons of cat mummies. Unbelievably, they were auctioned off as fertiliser at around £4 a ton! They had been discovered when a villager from Beni Hassan dug into the desert beyond the narrow fringe of Nile cultivation and found hundreds of thousands of cat mummies packed in layers twenty deep.

The only Egyptologist to visit the site was William Martin Conway, who wrote:

In modern Egypt as at the time of the pharaohs, cats scavenge waste food from human settlements – here a mackerel tabby finds what it can in the narrow streets of the Cairo bazaar. Was scavenging around man the route to domestication thousands of years ago?

THE CULT OF THE CAT

The plundering of the cemetery was a sight to see, but one had to stand well to windward. The village children came from day to day and provided themselves with the most attractive mummies they could find. These they took down to the river bank to sell for the smallest coin to passing travellers. The path became strewn with mummy cloth and bits of cats' skulls and bones and fur in horrid profusion, and the wind blew the fragments about and carried the stink afar.

Local contractors used the bones for tooth powder, while the wrappings were taken away for manure. Conway took from the site one of the few bronzes found there; it had contained a mummy of what he believed was in its day the principal cat at Pakhet's shrine.

Undisturbed for thousands of years, this great mass of preserved cats was discovered just a few years too soon. After museums and collectors had acquired a few special pieces they were not interested in the huge amount of material that remained. Today, a careful evaluation of the mummies would have revealed much about the early days of the domestic cat. Amazingly, only one skull from the 19½ ton shipment survives at the British Museum.

More recently, at the temple of Pakhet I found large numbers of fragments of cat bones, many of them charred. The rooms where I came across them are now inhabited by bats, but probably once contained temple cats. Among these bones were those of the jungle cat, so the nearby early tomb painting depicting this species was right.

From the few skulls measured in the last century and this it has been suggested that the cats mummified after domestication included the jungle cat and the African wild cat; but the majority were of another cat, between these two in size, which was termed *Felis lybica bubastis*. So what was *bubastis* – a halfway house to the present-day

The plundering of cat cemeteries in the past, here reconstructed for the TV series, has resulted in vast quantities of mummies being destroyed which would have been an invaluable aid to unearthing the cat's route to domestication.

smaller cat? As it seems to have been larger than the African wild cat this could give credibility to the concept of the Ancient Egyptians producing a temple hybrid. If only males were mummified, that would make sense of the measurements; perhaps the females were cremated. The basic problem is that we haven't had enough mummies available from known sites to make real sense of the origin of the cat.

What is the conclusion?

The true origin of the domestic cat may, I feel, lie in a compromise between the two theories. It is quite probable that bolder individuals of the African wild cat did exploit the food resources of the emerging small settlements, but that hybridising with the jungle cat at temple sites modified the new animal. It is also possible

The author at the temple of Pakhet, examining a find at the exciting seam of cat mummies he uncovered there during the making of the series. Will this new evidence at last provide the true story of the domestication of the cat?

that a cross between the African wild cat and the jungle cat at a temple site produced tamer individuals that were more amenable to man, that these were bred from and then strayed to the new towns.

In 1982 there was a great breakthrough. Alain Zivie, a French archaeologist working on Vizir Aperia's tomb at Saqqara, a huge 'city of the dead' in the desert beyond the west bank of the Nile, found thousands of cat mummies heaped in its tunnels and shafts. The significance of his find was that, unusually, the mummies were the normal run-of-the-mill type, just bound in rough bandaging. It will take many years for a full investigation of this multitude of finds from the Ptolemaic and subsequent periods, but they should reveal much information. Yet as Saqqara was a necropolis rather than a cult centre like Bubastis or Pakhet's temple at Beni Hassan, which should have held some remains from earlier years of cat domestication, it was particularly unfortunate that these had been mined out in the nineteenth century.

Then, during the making of the TV series on which this book is based, I was amazed to discover a whole new seam of cat mummies at Pakhet's temple; for a hundred years it had been believed that Pakhet's cemeteries had been completely lost. The seam runs for two hundred feet and consists of a nine-inch-thick layer of compressed mummies, dark brown with decaying wrappings in stark contrast to the intact protruding bones and surrounding pale stones.

Now, with these new finds of 'everyday' mummies, it may be possible to work out what really happened. As the temple site of Pakhet is a contender for the site of domestication, these bones could at last offer the key to a full understanding of the origins of the domestic cat.

Left *An early representation of the domestic cat as a pet: Roman grave stele of the first or second century AD, depicting a child with a cat and a chicken. From excavations at Colchester it would seem that cats and chickens were introduced to Britain together, via Roman trade.*

Opposite *In the border of a medieval manuscript a cat plays a fiddle.*

2 The Cat Arrives in Europe

After 30 BC, when Cleopatra's navy was defeated, Egypt became a Roman province. At that time the Roman Empire accepted a diverse range of cults, and continued to do so until some four hundred years later, when the Emperor Theodosius declared Christianity to be the state religion. All others were suppressed, including the worship of Bastet. Without the cult that had contained it in Egypt, the cat moved further afield.

A nursery rattle

When the cat first spread to Europe it still had divine status, and the sistrum accompanied it. This four-runged instrument was probably the basis for medieval portrayals of cats playing fiddles, such as the carving of a cat with four kittens on a choir stall at Beverley Minster, which carries a strong echo of Bastet. And the ancient nursery rhyme of uncertain origin makes more sense if we associate it with the sistrum:

> Hey diddle diddle
> The cat and the fiddle
> The cow jumped over the moon.

It then becomes a distant legacy of the ancient fertility

31

rites at Bubastis, with all the elements present: the cat goddess Bastet, the sistrum, the cow goddess Hathor, and the moon.

The virgin-mother goddesses

All the religions of the Mediterranean had a mother earth goddess figure who was both eternally virginal and at the same time the essence of fertility. Bastet fulfilled this role in Egypt, as did Artemis in Greece and Diana for the Romans. For Herodotus, Alexander the Great and their Greek contemporaries, Bastet and Artemis were different forms of the same deity. Equally, Diana was recognised as synonymous with the cat goddess.

The same was true for the faiths of regions further north in Europe. Freyja performed this task for the tribes in present-day Germany and Scandinavia, while the Matres did so for the Celts. Ancient Teutonic myths tell of Freyja's chariot being drawn across the sky by small cats that are usually recorded as white but sometimes as black or grey. These colours show that domestic cats had arrived and been incorporated into northern European religions.

Just as the European faiths had transferred many of the attributes of Bastet to their own deities, so the early Christian Church actively absorbed cult festivals. The feast day of the virgin-mother goddess, Diana/Artemis, for instance, was overlaid by the celebration of the Assumption of the Virgin. The Virgin Mary became the inheritor of the virgin-mother goddess traditions.

Leonardo da Vinci's sketch of the Holy Family with a cat. Here the animal symbolises the divine fertility of the Virgin Mary.

The Cat and the Virgin Mary

From the thirteenth century onwards there was an upsurge in religious paintings of the Virgin and Child, which was to become a familiar image in Western art.

33

Some of these pictures, such as the sixteenth-century Italian painter Lorenzo Lotto's *Annunciation*, include a cat. In Lotto's picture, as the Virgin is informed of her pregnancy a cat runs across the floor. Art historians often assert that this represents the devil fleeing at the sight of the angel – but surely if a cat flees from an angel it would not be a fit companion for the 'Mother of God'? If that was the symbolism of a cat with the Holy Family, as seen by medieval and Renaissance artists, then the Christ child would not be lovingly hugging the cat as in Leonardo da Vinci's tender sketch. These cats stand for the divine fertility of the Virgin, and as such are a direct descendant of Bastet, the essence of fertility.

In addition to this symbolism the Copts, the original Christians in Egypt, believed that when the Holy Family fled to Egypt to escape Herod's slaughter of infants they stayed for a while at Bubastis. This was at the height of cat worship, so perhaps Mary and the young Christ child did play with cats, and the subject of Leonardo's sketch may have been a true story.

The Annunciation, by Lorenzo Lotto. Is the devil, in the form of a cat, fleeing from the angel – or, as is more likely, is the cat intended as a fertility symbol?

The Phoenicians and the black cat

Egyptian domestic cats had the striped pattern of their wild ancestors, but soon after they emerged from their country of origin the first coat colour mutation occurred – the black cat appeared. The geneticist Neil Todd traced the spread of the black cat to the Phoenicians, a trading people based between about 1200 and 146 BC in what are now Lebanon and Syria, but with trading centres elsewhere in the Mediterranean. The mutation probably occurred in one of their North African ports and spread with their trade (see pp. 97–9 for an explanation of the genetic changes involved).

THE CULT OF THE CAT

It is sometimes said that the first domestic cats to arrive in Britain were black ones carried by the Phoenicians, but these seafarers had no established direct links with Britain. Their trade in British tin seems to have been carried out via Spain and the Celts, and the black cat may have arrived by this means. Yet it was probably with the regular shipping of the Romans that the domestic cat first came to the shores of Britain.

The first British cats

Stand in the vaults of the Temple of Claudius in Colchester and you feel you are back in the first capital of Roman Britain. It was built by the Romans to honour their Emperor of that name who invaded Britain in AD 43, triumphantly entering Celtic Colchester at the head of an army made doubly impressive by elephants. Previously it had been Britain's main 'city', and its recently deceased king, Cunobelin, had traded extensively with the Romans who knew him as *Rex Britannicus*.

As evidence of this trade, bones from the first chicken recorded in Britain were found in a defensive ditch in Cunobelin's Colchester. A single cat bone was found alongside, but until now its significance has been overlooked. I believe this to be the earliest remains of a domestic cat to have been found in Britain; it is datable to AD 10–43, just before the Roman invasion. The bones of wild and domestic cats are notoriously difficult to distinguish: but the site, and what is found with them, can help identification. Earlier cat bones have been excavated, but, because of the range of wild animal bones found with them, they are probably those of the wild *Felis silvestris*. At Colchester the farmyard stock, the nature of the site and the bone's size all strongly suggest a domestic cat.

'And did those feet, in ancient time . . . ?' Roman tiles from Chelmsford, Essex, bearing the clear imprint of a cat's paws.

From Roman Chelmsford I have identified a number of roof tiles impressed with cats' paw prints. It is unlikely that a wild cat would walk across the local tile-drying yard, among human habitation, but it is exactly the sort of thing a domestic cat does – as anyone knows who has just laid a concrete path! Four of these cat prints were used as footings for the foundations of a third-century temple, probably as we might bury coins in foundations today for good luck.

In domestic settings at the third-century Roman coastal fort of Porchester the remains of many cats have been excavated, including entire skeletons found in particular wells. Beside a temple in Roman Chelmsford a ritual well contained horse skulls and cat bones dated about AD 150. The Celts saw water emerging from a hole in the ground as an entrance to the other world, and these were sacrifices to the mother fertility goddess.

Demonic fusion

Few Roman soldiers at this late stage were from Rome itself; most were mercenaries from the various parts of the Empire. This mixture of peoples hastened the blending of faiths, linking the mother earth fertility deities, including the cat, and amalgamating the potent male horned figures, like the half goat Pan which was prevalent in cultures dependent on grazing.

Once Christianity had become the religion of the Empire, all others were termed 'pagan' and their gods relegated to the world of demons and devils. Pan figures became the male devil, while Diana figures like the cat became demonic. Followers of other religions were castigated as devil worshippers.

Christianity became a male-dominated creed with few

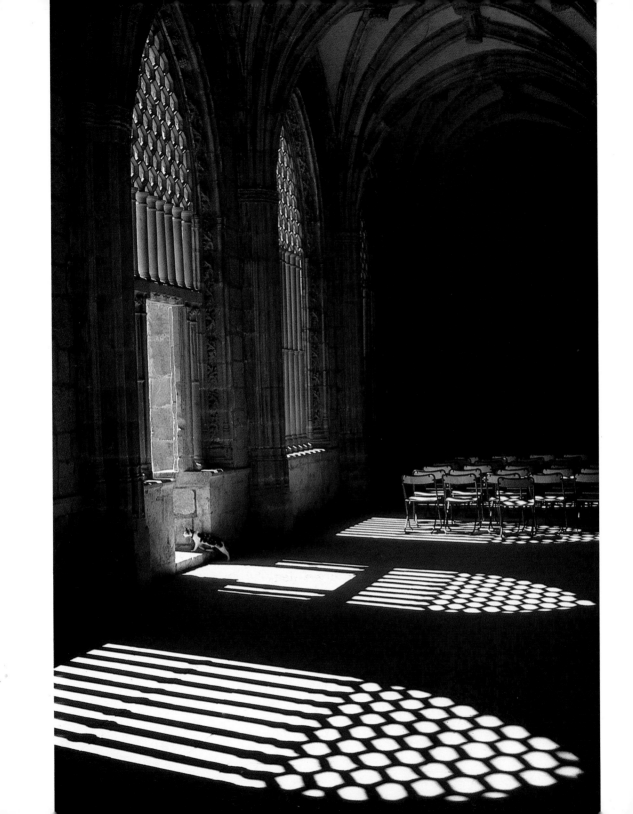

In the past monasteries provided cats with shade in the heat of the day, warmth and shelter in cold weather, and always abundant waste food from the kitchens.

roles for women apart from those of subservient acolytes: small wonder that women who believed in their local faiths were not drawn into an alien, imposed Church. With increasing opposition and time the old fertility faiths degenerated. Witchcraft would emerge.

The cat escapes

Under the Roman occupation the cat lived in forts and towns, and as the treasured pet of the new ruling class in their country villas. But when pressure from invading hordes grew at home, the occupying forces were gradually withdrawn to defend Rome. In the fifth century the last of the Romans left Britain and their cats were abandoned to live feral.

Britain was now prey to other invaders. As the Saxons began to cultivate more and more of the land, the forest was supplanted by fields and the feral cat, now exploiting human habitation, supplanted the forest wild cat. As villages developed, so did the domestic cat population. But the cat was seen as a working animal, not as a fireside pet; its value was based on size and usefulness, as shown by laws enacted in 936 by Hywel the Good, Prince of South Wales. A kitten was worth a penny until it opened its eyes, then twopence until it caught its first mouse, when it was worth fourpence. If a cat guarding the corn in the royal barn was killed, the amount of wheat due in compensation was decided in this way: the dead cat was held by its tail so that its head just touched the ground, and then wheat was poured in a heap until the tip of the tail was covered.

THE CULT OF THE CAT

Monastery moggies

Initially cats were accepted as strays around monasteries. Just as today hospital sites encourage the development of feral cat groups, so medieval monasteries had warm, central kitchens producing plenty of waste food, and a complex of buildings which offered protection from the weather. As today individual nurses will put out food for cats, so some monks struck up friendships with certain cats. An Irish monastic scholar in the eighth or ninth century doted on his, and wrote a poem to celebrate their relationship:

> *I and Pangur Ban, my cat*
> *'Tis a like task we are at;*
> *Hunting mice is his delight*
> *Hunting words I sit all night,*
> *So in peace our tasks we ply,*
> *Pangur Ban, my cat, and I.*

Cats were popular with the early Celtic Irish Church. As the Romans did not reach Ireland it may be the monks who took the first black and tabby cats there, but the ginger ones probably arrived later, with the Vikings.

A very matter-of-fact attitude prevailed during the early medieval period. When cat numbers became too many they were simply culled, as at Essex's Bicknacre Priory where the hunting of cats was given the official approval of King Henry III in a royal charter; cat was the only fur that ecclesiastics were permitted to wear. It used to be supposed that only true wild cats were hunted, yet the medieval chase term 'a clowder of cats' refers to a group; this is far more applicable to the hunting of ferals than of the more solitary wild cats.

Magic and myth

Sir Richard Whittington, thrice Lord Mayor of London. In the sixteenth century the image of the cat as a bringer of good luck, as in the story of Dick Whittington, co-existed with its perceived more sinister role as witch's familiar and instrument of evil.

By the medieval period, although the cat had lost its divine status for most people, it was still believed to have magic powers. Having a cat for 'good luck' was not passive, but was thought to cause the luck in some way. The tales of Dick Whittington and Puss in Boots which form the basis of today's Christmas pantomimes were written down in the seventeenth century, but originated in the traditional stories of magic cats aiding their masters to good fortune which dated back to early medieval times.

The pantomime story of Dick Whittington tells of a poor boy's rise to wealth and power as Lord Mayor of London, helped by a cat. The real Whittington did make a fortune and become Lord Mayor of London, yet there is no evidence that he ever owned a cat. The first known picture of him with a cat was made over a hundred years after his death but only thirty years before the first English witchcraft trials. The artist was probably illustrating the commonly held belief that a sudden rise in fortune was due to magical intervention, and that meant a cat.

These tales represent the positive side of cat magic, seen for once by the perpetrators rather than the persecutors. Equally positive was the practice of interring cats in the walls of houses to keep away rats and evil; it survived until the end of the nineteenth century. However, to the medieval mind there was a sinister side to cat magic, associated with demons and witchcraft. It led to the lowest ebb in the history of the cat.

3 From Witch's Familiar to Pampered Pet

Ieper, city of cats

Every year for one day an entire city celebrates the cat – a massive procession is staged in which thousands of people dress up as cats of all shapes and sizes. Ieper in Belgium, better known as Ypres, was devastated during World War I but then rebuilt as before, including the famous Cloth Hall with its 230-foot-high tower. The place has also kept alive its ancient Cats' Festival and parade that winds for hours through the streets.

The entire history of the cat passes before your eyes: a statue of Bastet on a state barge is followed by the Black Cat of Connaught, the Irish Celtic cat noted for its dreadful oracles. The Germanic fertility goddess Freyja, seated twenty feet up in the air, is pulled along by two enormous pussy cats. Then a huge Knight Templar symbolises the key point in the destiny of cats, when their acceptance by society turned sour. Now the parade enters the era of witchcraft and the degradation of cats: a witch trial is followed by leaping flames as witches are 'burnt'. But why do over 2000 people dress up every year and take to the streets to tell the story of the cat?

The origin lies in the ritual after the procession. The year's Cat Queen, her attendants and jester ascend the Cloth Tower, from which the jester throws out cats – to

Every May the people of Ieper in Belgium dress up and parade through the city streets, past the famous Cloth Hall, in commemoration of a centuries-old ritual in which cats were thrown from a high tower.

THE CULT OF THE CAT

the delight of the crowd below. Nowadays only toys are thrown, but up until 1817 live cats were used.

This bizarre ritual is a symbolic re-enactment of an event that first took place a thousand years ago. In 962 the Count of Ypres and joint-Count of Flanders, Baldwin III, ordered two or three cats to be thrown from a tower built on a cult shrine of a brass cat with two kittens. It has been said that the purpose was to convince accusers that Ieper had ceased to worship cats; but the tenth century was early for accusations of this kind, and had the citizens wished to destroy cats in public the animals could have been burnt, drowned, crushed or beaten with flails.

In 1817 the keeper of the town records noted:

As in the past, the person entrusted with this task threw down into the crowd the animal which they wished to sacrifice, and which sometimes in spite of the height of the fall, was not at all hurt, and ran off quickly so that it might never be caught again for a similar ceremony.

I believe that, rather than a public demonstration of the abandonment of cat worship, the tower ritual was seen as a proof of the cat's supernatural powers. Its miraculous ability to fall from a great height and land safely on its feet was certainly known by around 1260, from this description by a Franciscan friar, Bartholomeus

Above A fifteenth-century misericord from the church of St Sulpice at Diest in Belgium depicts a man in the act of throwing a cat.
Below left and right
This famous sequence of photographs taken by the French physiologist Marey in 1894 shows the stages by which a thrown or falling cat rights itself by the time it hits the ground. This ability allows cats to survive very long falls – injured, admittedly, but alive.

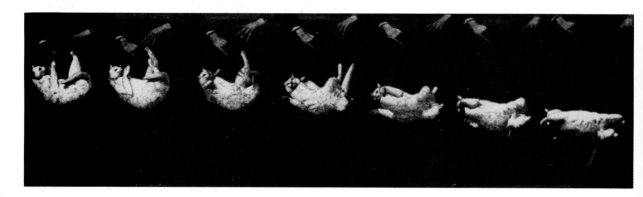

Anglicus, of what could be the annual cat-throwing in Ieper: 'and unneth is hurt when he is thrown down off an high place'.

Free-falling cats

Exactly how a cat rights itself was first demonstrated in 1894 by photographs taken at the rate of sixty per second by the French physiologist Marey. Immediately on falling, the cat rotates its front half and brings its head upright; then a twist turns the hind quarters. When the cat is the right way up its limbs extend, anticipating its landing. The animal spreads out horizontally to an extent, increasing drag and slowing the rate of descent. Cats can thus survive falling incredible distances. Recently an amazing 90 per cent of cats falling from New York skyscrapers were found to have survived, though suffering injuries. Unexpectedly, those falling more than 85 feet stood a better chance, as their rotations were more stabilised before landing.

It is a survival adaptation that is useful when racing along branches after prey, as a tumble occasionally

Right *With today's photo-graphic equipment Marey's falling cat would have resembled this multi-image picture of the same subject.*

Leaping and balancing are two skills for which the cat is supremely well adapted, as demonstrated by this Blue Burmese.

happens in the heat of the chase. This, like its reflective eyes, was a feature of the cat's woodland nocturnal hunter background that medieval man misunderstood – to the detriment of the cat. If a man, dog or cow was thrown from a high tower, they died; yet cats could fall all that distance and many, apparently miraculously, ran off unhurt. No wonder the crowds thronged to watch.

46

Cats seem able to balance
effortlessly and motionlessly
on the smallest and meanest of
perches, a very useful facility
when observing and stalking
prey that lives in trees.

The sinister swing

The cat's acceptance in Europe underwent a dramatic change as a result of fundamental shifts in social and religious outlooks during the thirteenth century. As tolerance died, so did the cat – in its thousands.

During the era of the crusades, which began in the eleventh century, Christian and Muslim scholars discoursed in Spain and the Middle East. The warm South of France, from Aquitaine to Provence, was particularly receptive to new ideas, including that of 'courtly love', which idealised women. Provençal culture at that time was amongst the most sophisticated in Europe. Intriguingly, a female saint of the south, St Agatha, was spoken of in the Languedoc as Santo Gato – Saint Cat.

The powerful women of the Languedoc encouraged the rise of new religious sects like the Cathars or Albigensians (named after the town of Albi), which in common with the early Christian Church preached the merits of purity and simplicity in daily life. They synthesised Christianity with the teachings of the Persian prophet Mani, and with mystical and metaphysical elements that were not part of official Catholicism. Mani's followers had been accused of worshipping a black cat; in third-century Babylon the prophet had fused a number of local religions and had had contact with cat worship in the nearby Egyptian delta. The twelfth-century scholar Alain de Lille declared that the Cathars were named after cats, for that was how Lucifer appeared to them. And some members of a similar sect, the Waldensians, 'confessed' to a cat being involved in certain ceremonies, and to kissing it under the tail.

These breakaway sects were soon declared heretical by mainstream Christians who were suspicious of the over-

The frantic, boisterous games kittens play are instinctive behaviour – a rehearsal for the more serious matter of catching prey once they are skilled enough.

tones of paganism and devil worship. Pope Innocent III instigated the ruthless Albigensian Crusade and the Inquisition to deal with these popular movements, and in so doing he also destroyed Provençal culture.

The Templars

The Knights Templar were a noble order of fighting monks formed in 1119 to provide safe passage for pilgrims to the Holy Land. Their impeccable honour encouraged the princes of Europe to use them as bankers and to safeguard valuables, but the wealth that the Templars accrued by this means lost them popularity. In addition, living permanently in the Middle East enabled them to develop a familiarity with their neighbours in other cultures, and this 'contamination' by Eastern religions, manners and customs made them suspect to the rest of Europe.

In 1291 all Christians were driven from the Holy Land, and a third of the 15,000 Templars became based in France. This wealthy standing army, over which he had no control, unnerved King Philip the Fair of France, who induced the Grand Inquisitor to denounce them as heretics and to extract 'confessions' under torture. The Templars were accused of renouncing Christ and worshipping idols. Some 'admitted' to worshipping a black cat idol, and to kissing a cat during services; the idol was called Baphomet, a very similar name to Bastet. These 'confessions' were sufficient excuse for the King of France to destroy the Order.

Were these accusations complete nonsense? The Templars had lived in a region perfused by the ideas of the ancient cat cult of Egypt, and containing far more cats than Europe. These monks, living in isolation, were

In the medieval mind, 'heretics' were often associated with weird practices involving that suspect creature the cat. This illustration from the Book of Maccabees in the late twelfth-century Winchester Bible shows Mattathias beheading an idolater. Such images of cat worship were drawn from the topical furore that arose in Europe over the Cathar heresy.

probably charmed by what to them was a relatively unusual animal; as some Templar castles lay in the mountainous border country of what is today Turkey, the Order may have introduced the earliest Angoras to France. It is unlikely, however, that the Templars had cat connections of the kind suspected by the Inquisition. Nevertheless such were the prevailing attitudes that it became standard to accuse heretics of such practices.

Burning cats

Not only were people persecuted for their presumed profane relations with cats; the cats themselves were victims. The Celts had sought to ensure the continuity of the life force by ritually burning manifestations of their deities. The Celtic midsummer festival of sacrifice fires, in which cats were burnt as objects of veneration, became adopted as the Christian feast of St John's Day. But the fire sacrifices continued, demonstrating a recognition of the divine in the cat, although demonic.

The late Middle Ages became a time of unspeakable cruelty to cats, which were burnt alive in their thousands. Throughout Europe they were roasted in wicker cages above bonfires, to prolong their agony and to make the devil suffer. At the accession of the anti-Catholic Elizabeth I in 1558 street mobs in London burned effigies of the Pope containing cats: they were supposed to symbolise him as the Antichrist or the devil, with whom the cat had become synonymous. Public attitudes did not change until the mid-seventeenth century, when King Louis XIV became the last French monarch to kindle the Midsummer Fire in Paris.

THE CULT OF THE CAT

The rise of witchcraft

With the development of villages, some feral cats struck up relationships with lonely widows. Both suffered when tolerance gave way to hysterical persecution. The women were accused of witchcraft, and the cats were regarded as devils.

Myth portrays witches riding at night on broomsticks to meet in groups known as covens, where they took part naked in magic rituals. These are the witches of the powerful paintings of the Spanish court painter Goya, and of Shakespeare's three potion-stirrers on their blasted heath in *Macbeth*. In Britain the hotbed of witchcraft was the fiercely Protestant county of Essex, where the cat had first arrived in the country. The witch-hunting frenzy reached its peak between 1580 and 1590, when 13 per cent of all indictments at the county assizes were for witchcraft.

Medieval misunderstanding

But although we now think of witches as caricature grotesques, earlier they were taken seriously by the Church. Such women, usually elderly, were often guardians of ancient traditions and adherents of the virgin-mother goddess beliefs, and would welcome the cat as an echo of Bastet. That perception was shared by their accusers, and the same misunderstandings of the cat's biology that made the Egyptians deify it now caused it to be vilifed as a demon.

The glowing, light-reflective eyes of the cat are caused by a crystal mirror layer behind the retina, which doubles the cat's chance of seeing something in low light conditions. Such features are ideal for the night and woodland hunter, but to witch persecutors they were demonic 'eies [that] glister . . . and in the night they can hardly be endured for their flaming aspect,' as Edward Topsell recorded in his *Historie of Foure-Footed Beasts*. Another reason for the medieval misunderstanding of the cat originated in observations of breeding animals at the Ancient Egyptian cat temples. In AD 120 the Roman naturalist Aelian wrote of a tom cat: '. . . the semen which he ejaculates is exceedingly hot and like fire, and burns the female organ'. This was reiterated by later writers, and as Topsell in the early seventeenth century phrased it: '. . . his seed is so fiery hot, that it almost burneth the female places of conception'.

It is easy to understand why this belief arose, for as the male leaves the female after mating she yowls and strikes at him. The real reason is no less dramatic than the mythical one. The tom cat has barbs on his penis which rake the vaginal wall as he withdraws; these spines are not some demonic apparatus, but are linked to the cat's social system. Males of the female's group are around when her

The female cat's apparently vicious response to the tom immediately after mating has a straightforward physical cause, which reduces inbreeding. Not understood until relatively recently, this was one of the reasons why the cat was seen for centuries as a demonic creature.

hormones bring her 'into season', but unlike most mammals she does not release her eggs with her hormonal cycle. Instead, the raking of the vagina at the first mating releases the eggs, which then travel down the tubes to the uterus. This allows time for interested males from other groups to arrive, thus reducing inbreeding. Her behaviour changes from being quite unfriendly at the first mating into that of a demanding 'cat on heat'.

The lustful behaviour and multiple matings that characterise the sexual activities of cats were seen in medieval and Tudor times as a sign of ungodliness. The cat's own natural instincts were turned against it, and became a further nail in its coffin during this age of fear and narrow-mindedness.

Victims of superstitious minds

Both Protestant and Catholic Churches attacked those unfortunate social outsiders, the cat and the 'witch'. The first major English witchcraft trial took place in Essex in 1565. Here the cat as 'familiar' emerged for the first time – the carrying out of witches' requests by familiars was a peculiarly British phenomenon. Elizabeth I's Attorney General appeared as prosecutor at this trial, indicating how seriously the state viewed the matter.

Cats know beforehand when it is going to rain, and wash over their ears at such times. In the past, this and other weather-connected activities were misinterpreted – cats were believed actually to cause a change in the weather, and such powers were perceived as dangerous.

The case against Elizabeth Francis, Agnes Waterhouse and her daughter Joan revolved around the ownership of a cat. According to the trial records, Elizabeth learned the 'arte of witchcraft' at the age of twelve from her grandmother, who told her 'to geue of her bloudde to Sathan whyche she delyuered her in the lykenesse of a whyte spotted Catte . . . she taughte her to cal it by the name of Sathan'. In due course, after making various requests of the animal including the killing of her lover and her own

Margaret,   Joan Flower,   Philipa,

Her two Daughters.

From the mid-sixteenth century the witch-hunting frenzy in England led to a number of trials, in which otherwise perfectly ordinary women who happened to own cats were accused of using these 'familiars' to do evil to others.

child, Elizabeth gave the cat to her neighbour, Mother Waterhouse. The new owner caused the cat to kill other neighbours' livestock, then a neighbour 'with a bludye flixe', and finally her own husband.

Elizabeth Francis was given a year's imprisonment. Joan Waterhouse gave evidence and was released. But her mother was found guilty of 'bewitching to death' and was executed. In this case, otherwise ordinary women were portrayed as receiving withcraft power by association with the cat.

In 1582 another trial took place at Chelmsford; it introduced the idea of a group of witches operating together in a coven with a number of familiars. Thirteen women from St Osyth were accused of bewitching twenty-three people to death. Instead of looking for some disease that might have cut short these villagers' lives, the local lord of the manor was convinced the infection was witchcraft.

The court heard about strange familiars including miniature cows, but cats were in the majority. One of the accused, Mother Peachy, had a kitten, and this alone led to her imprisonment despite her denial of the charges. Cicely Celles was condemned for having a 'white imp' in the form of a cat which 'pricked Alice Baxter to the heart', and for having 'witch marks' – it was believed that witches suckled their familiars with their own blood, and so they were searched for 'witch marks', which could be something as ordinary as a mole. The defendants were asked whether they kept wool in a basket as a bed for familiars. Alice Manfield confessed that twelve years earlier she had been given four cats, which she kept on wool in a box. The judge believed kindness to cats to be most suspect.

As the trials continued, the myths grew. Cats detect in advance when it is likely to rain, and wash over their ears; they also dash about in blustery weather. This connection between feline behaviour and weather was misinterpreted by the superstitious minds of those times: the cat was felt actually to cause the weather to change. The most famous case was that of Agnes Sampson. Under torture she 'admitted' that, along with other witches, she had performed a ritual with a cat in order to create a storm to sink the ship bearing King James I and Queen Anne from Denmark to Scotland.

The reputation of cats became so debased that their persecution and casual torture grew to be a part of everyday life. In Brussels in 1549, for instance, the visiting Spanish king was entertained by a grotesque cat organ, on which live cats' tails were pulled when the keys were struck.

THE CULT OF THE CAT

The dawn of enlightenment

During the mid-eighteenth century the cat started to become more acceptable again. Independent-minded people like the literary Dr Johnson began its rehabilitation by example, owning a number of cats; the actor manager John Rich lived with 'seven and twenty cats of all sizes, colours and kinds'. Yet in his *Stages of Cruelty* prints the artist Hogarth portrayed the typical abuse of cats, and vicious 'teasing' by small boys, that was still prevalent.

Cat and dog: misinterpreted behaviour

Misunderstanding of the cat's temperament and behaviour caused it problems for many centuries. Its independence has always been recognised, so it is not strange that those seeking power and total obedience, such as assertive kings and princes of the Church, should frequently have loathed them. The stereotypical cat hater remains the authoritarian, while the cat lover is more tolerant.

Since medieval times the dog has been seen as an honest friend, while the cat was regarded as suspect and untrustworthy. From the evidence of centuries of art across Europe, the dog has been at least ten times more popular than the cat. But given the paranoia that surrounded witchcraft that is not surprising.

It is remarkable that both the cat and the dog came to share our lives, considering their disparate biological backgrounds. The wild ancestors of the dog evolved in open landscape where pack hunting by sight, picking off single animals from herds, is a natural strategy. Group hunting of this kind demands a social structure and hierarchy established through aggression.

In contrast the cat's ancestors evolved in woodlands

Despite the cat's welcome acceptance at some levels of society, its abuse and torture were still widespread in the eighteenth century when Hogarth made his series of prints known as the Stages of Cruelty *(detail).*

where stealthy hunting of individuals by individuals is more productive. Social interactions are irrelevant while hunting, and only significant in social settings, where affection is more appropriate than aggression.

Ironically, what generations of mankind have interpreted as loyal affection in the dog consists largely of displays of appeasing subservience to a pack leader. When the cat, so long maligned as 'aloof', shows affection it is

59

The expansion of towns and cities in the nineteenth century resulted in a rise in the population of feral cats, their night-time activities disturbing people's sleep as they prowled the alleyways and rooftops. The Cats' Meeting Place, a lithograph by the French artist Edouard Manet.

being friendly. Both animals respond according to their biological background, yet both fit into our world.

Rehabilitation at last

Despite the enlightened attitudes of some individuals from the eighteenth century onwards, the misunderstanding of the cat's true nature continued and for a long time the proportion of feral to house cats was far higher than it is today. Indeed, the expansion of towns and the creation of suburbs in Victorian times caused an increase in the feral cat population, as food sources multiplied. But by organising the first cat show in Britain in 1871 Harrison Weir sought to change public attitudes to the cat, and paved the way for its twentieth-century acceptance in our homes alongside the dog.

The Wild Side of Cats

Cats on the tiles in southern Spain.

A stone lion standing guard with a smaller cat at the gates of Venice's vast shipyard, the Arsenale.

4 The Social System of a Survivor

The cats of Venice

There are certain places around the world that will always be associated with cats, and Venice is one of them. From the winged lion that is the symbol of St Mark, the city's patron saint, to the ferals that walk alongside the green waterways and doze in the shade of the crumbling palazzos, the Venetian cats all have their devotees. Many of the elegant buildings have served their time as grain warehouses: the combination of rice, wheat and water was a perfect recipe for rats and mice. So the cats weren't just loved – they were needed!

At the gates of Venice's huge shipyard, the Arsenale, stand statues of lions pillaged from ancient sites around the Mediterranean. One was sent back by the great seventeenth-century admiral and Doge Francesco Morosini, who never travelled at sea without his pet cat. Morosini was not untypical, as indicated by the observations of John Locke, an English sailor who in 1553 was on a Venetian ship bound for the Holy Land when the ship's cat fell overboard.

The shippes Cat . . . kept her selfe very valiantly above water, the which the master knowing, he caused the Skiffe with halfe a dozen men to fetch her again, when she was almost halfe a mile from the shippe. I hardly believe they would have made such haste and meanes if one of the company had bene in the like

Wherever human habitation and feral cats coincide, someone will always be at hand to feed them. In his priest's cassock and biretta Don Fusaro is a familiar figure as he tends to his feline flock on the Venetian campi.

66

perill. This I have written onely to note the estimation the cats are in, among the Italians, for they esteeme their cattes, as in England we esteeme a good Spaniell.

Venice had strong trading links with Constantinople. It was likely, therefore, that it was on Venetian vessels that the first long-haired cats reached Europe from Turkey.

The continuing affection of Venetians for their cats is shown by the tale of Nini the Frari cat. For some years during the nineteenth century the peaceful Frari Square was inhabited by a large white tom cat called Nini, who regularly strolled between the café where he was fed and the Venetian State Archive building and Frari church alongside. The whimsical idea grew up that Nini was an especially worthy cat because of the time he spent in the church, and that he learned as he slept among the manu-scripts in the Archive. Among those cat lovers who signed their names in his visitors' book at the café were the Tsar of Russia, the Emperor of Ethiopia, the Pope and the com-poser Verdi, who not only wrote his name but also a few bars of his opera *La Traviata*.

Even today, you only have to step a few yards from the milling hubbub of St Mark's Square to the peace of the nearby public gardens and you are in the private domain of some twenty-five cats. Despite their nearness to the busy water's edge, the gardens provide a safe haven for these feral cats who are well fed by kind benefactors. Wherever it finds itself, the cat always makes the best use of available resources.

The feeders of feral cats

In cities feral cats obtain food by scavenging from rubbish skips and bins, but are also fed by kind-hearted people. In the centre of cities like London these are usually

Feeders of feral cats can be found right around the world, and they give the animals whatever they would offer their own house cats. These cats in Thailand are existing on a rice-based diet.

women, who develop a mutual dependence with a group of feral cats. The feeder sees cats that she believes need feeding, and the cats focus on a regular source of food. This happens the world over. In the bazaars of Cairo and Istanbul, among the stalls and in the shadows of mosques, it is usually men who feed the cats with raw or tinned meat. In Athens it is often the left-overs that are given, while in Bangkok the feral cats have a rice-based

diet. In Britain and America it is normally tinned food that is provided. Each society gives feral cats what it gives its own house cats.

Home on the range

'Feral' is a term applied to an animal that was once domesticated but has reverted to a wild state, or more properly has reverted from a domestic to a free-living state. In many cities like London house cats hold the private garden areas, while feral cats exist in the 'gaps' found at places like hospitals, factories and gardens in the centre of residential squares. In the mid-seventies, when I began a long-term study of feral cats in central London, I was one of only a handful of researchers throughout the world looking at the ranges and behaviour of cats living feral. In England David Macdonald and Peter Apps worked together on farm cats, while Jane Dards concentrated on those in docks. We found a certain pattern to cat ranges which has since been confirmed by researchers in other countries. From these studies it is clear that cat populations are higher when more food is about. Since it is more available to the urban street cat than to rural ferals and farm cats, cat densities are higher and home ranges smaller in towns and cities.

The tom's home range is usually around ten times the size of a female's, known as a queen. The size of the queen's home range is set by the amount of food she needs

Despite their hunting prowess cats will readily scavenge, and for urban feral cats that facility has often been essential for survival.

71

relative to how widely dispersed the food is. The tom's greater range is due not to a need for ten times as much food but to social reasons, so he can overlap a number of female ranges.

Where there is a regular food source, a number of cats will use it and their ranges will overlap, causing clumping of these ranges around the food area. Anyone who travels in the Mediterranean knows there can be a number of independent-living cats 'waiting at table'. You may also see numbers of cats scavenging on rubbish tips in many parts of the world. These cats are leading lives with a social structure: the area is home to them, and accommodates family and other cats of their group with which they lead a harmonious life. At Fitzroy Square, the central London area which I watched for many years, the cats were positively affectionate to one another, and the only real aggression was shown towards outsider cats.

When feral cats are fed at a regular time they anticipate the food's arrival, and in the ensuing close contact a lot of socialising occurs. Eating in Fitzroy Square would last up to three-quarters of an hour, though the most keen feeding took place in the first fifteen minutes. Cats would repeatedly acknowledge each other and the feeder by giving the 'tail up' greeting, and would rub against each other's heads and shoulders or against the iron railings.

Because the ranges of males are larger, individual female groups are isolated around the main food sources, with males providing a buffer zone between groups. This increases safety from marauding toms, and minimises the risk of kitten infections spreading. The social stability of the female group members, who are usually related, is seen in co-operative behaviour and suckling each other's kittens. These social benefits would be offset by inbreeding if mating only occurred within the group. Fortunately

Around the Mediterranean feral cats congregate at reliable sources of food such as cafés and tavernas, like this one in Turkey. Experience has taught them that if they catch the eye of some sympathetic customer or waiter they may get a morsel or two flung to them.

THE WILD SIDE OF CATS

The social behaviour of cat groups.
Below *Aggression is more usually shown towards outsiders – hardly ever towards members of the group.*

Opposite *Mock aggression and defensive postures are often struck in play between cats within a group, particularly among house cats.*

Below *Mutual grooming helps to cement the bond between two members of the same cat family or group.*

males also occasionally mate with females of adjacent groups.

A project begun in the 1970s in Nepal, which involved tracking tigers by means of radio transmitters, showed that in this respect these big forest cats are like the domestic cat: male tigers have a big range overlapping a number of smaller female ranges. The difference is that the females do not overlap on a common core area. Then in the 1980s a similar radiotracking study was done on European forest wild cats in north-eastern France; the results revealed the same range pattern as that of the tigers. If the wild cat was the main ancestor of the present domestic cat, why is the pattern similar but not identical? Was it a change that occurred around the time of domestication? No.

Feral domestic cats that live where they cannot scavenge from man, and where food is scarcer, have large ranges; they also tend not to clump their ranges. On the Galapagos Islands in the Pacific Ocean (see page 89), and on Heisker, an uninhabited island in the Outer Hebrides, the queens hardly overlap at all. Where feral domestic cats have to hunt widely for all their food, the range pattern is identical with that of wild cats. If there is a food source such as a bird colony, the ranges overlap more. The domestic cats on the Hebridean island of North Uist, for instance, have ranges that overlap around rabbit warrens where they catch prey.

So feral domestic cats have the same range pattern as true wild cats, and females' ranges do not clump where food is not abundant but is spread out. But where feral cats can exploit a plentiful local food source they do clump their ranges and gain the social advantages that this brings.

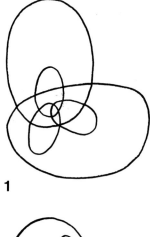

1

2

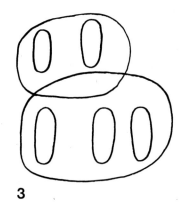

3

Cat alongside man

Mankind's population explosion over the last century has been accompanied by cats. In much of Britain, Europe and North America they have become 'lap cats', as suburban as wall-to-wall carpeting, yet it is not so round most of the world.

In the villages of the Spanish Pyrenees, for instance, the cats are not primarily pets, even though cat holes are cut in house doors for access. Here they are invaluable rodent controllers, playing a semi-feral, semi-farm cat role even though living around a house. The same situation can be found from the hill villages of Turkey to the Terai jungle of Nepal, where cats live usefully alongside man without being pampered.

The suburban house cat

The home ranges of cats: the larger loops in these diagrams represent the ranges of males, the smaller ones those of females.
1 The clumped ranges of feral cats where they are exploiting a plentiful local source of food.
2 The normal range pattern of tigers and forest wild cats. This is also the pattern of feral cats when food is dispersed and scarce.
3 The home ranges of house cats.

If you have a female cat you can see that she has a most definite home range which usually corresponds to your garden and a little more. Just as with feral cats, if your cat is male he will have a larger range – about ten times that of a queen, though usually a little less if he is neutered. Well-fed suburban house cats have smaller ranges than ferals. The house cat pattern makes sense when you appreciate that in many ways your cat relates to you as it does to another cat: you and your family are members of its group.

To your queen, the interior of your house is the equivalent of a feral cat's group core area. Since you are regarded as group members, your use of the garden when weeding or mowing the lawn reassures her about the extent of her range. If you don't make much use of your garden, neither will your female cat. Her range, which consists of paths,

Above *'Chinning' – leaving a scent produced by glands under the chin – is one method of marking a territory or leaving signals for other cats.* Opposite *Favourite snoozing spots are key features of a cat's range. Some are in warm, sunny places, while others are cooler.*

and snoozing spots in sun and shade, is marked out by scent. Cats have scent glands under their chins, on their heads and along their backs. They leave scents by 'chinning' and rubbing against objects, and investigate scents left by other cats. By rubbing against us, our cat gives us a group scent identity.

If your cat is a tom he identifies with your family as his main group and food source, but he sets his home range size relative to the local queens' range size. If your tom has not been neutered, in addition to other scent marking activities he will spray urine. It is the undeniable pungency of a tom's spray, as much as a sense of social responsibility about not allowing unwanted kittens to be conceived, that encourages their owners to have them neutered.

Cat–human communication

Our cats respond to us as if we too were cats. Much of their interaction with us can be thought of as extensions of juvenile behaviour – but then so can ours for playing with them. However, not all cat–human interaction can be seen only in that light.

When a cat which you are stroking kneads your jumper, it is using part of its kitten-instinct repertoire: your stroking reminds it of its mother's tongue, and kneading the mother's flank stimulates the flow of milk. When your cat meets you and you put your hand down to stroke its back, it lifts its tail in greeting and rubs around you as it would with another member of a cat group. If you repeatedly stroke your cat, running your hand down its back, it will raise its rump and go into the pre-mating position, known as lordosis. In contact between human beings, stroking is normally reserved for sexual contact of a pre-mating form. So when we stroke a cat, both our behaviour and the cat's response would be perceived sexually in another context – yet as it is, we are just conveying affection within the restrictions imposed by our ability to communicate with each other.

So the cat sees us as a member of its society at several levels: as mother/provider; as kitten (see below); even as potential sexual partner. Yet because we are so much larger the cat gains more warmth from human body

Our cats see us as members of their own society, but communication can be confusing: stroking has overtones of both kittenhood and adult sexual behaviour. Since human beings are so much larger than cats, such physical contact creates 'supernormal' stimuli.

contact than from contact with another cat, and more of its body will be covered by a stroke from a human hand than from a feline lick. We are in fact giving 'supernormal' stimuli. To a cat we are supercats – no wonder they are attracted to us!

Bringing in prey

Why does your cat bring in prey? Why doesn't it just eat it where it catches it? The cat is taking the prey back into the core area, which among feral cats carries the message that 'this is a good place to be'.

In our house 'core area' we must seem like intransigent kittens in need of training in the tender arts of catching and killing prey. A mother will bring her kittens first dead prey, then maimed prey and finally live prey; this is known as prey display. She does not just present it, but acts as a competitor, which encourages the young to take part.

My own two cats provide a good example of how over a period of time prey display can improve the hunting expertise of members of a cat's immediate social group. Leroy, a tabby and white moggie, was a young, streetwise urban stray when I acquired him. In his first year with me he brought in over 150 items of prey, of which – unusually for a cat – 80 were frogs. Tabitha, on the other hand, came to me as a kitten with no hunting coaching from her mother, and over the same year caught only a few butterflies, spiders and bees. Leroy has frequently played with a catch near Tabitha until she grabs it when unguarded; she then becomes a demented banshee, growling at anyone who might do the same to her. Watching Leroy's actions has gradually introduced her to eating and now catching and killing small mammals and birds.

In normal circumstances a mother will gradually teach her kittens, by example, how to deal with prey. If a kitten has been parted from its mother before these important prey display activities have taken place, it can still learn from watching another more experienced cat.

When cats bring prey into the house it often causes us concern. But on rare occasions this habit has proved to be a life-saver for the owner. Around 1480 a nobleman named Sir Henry Wyat was imprisoned by King Richard III and thrown into a dungeon to starve. A cat found her way in; he befriended her, and she took up residence there. From time to time the cat brought home a pigeon, which Wyat had his jailer cook for him, and thus he managed to stay alive until he secured his release after the death of his royal enemy.

What cats catch

In a recent study a schoolteacher, Peter Churcher, asked all his neighbours in the 173-household English village of Felmersham to collect the prey that their cats brought home. Over one year the seventy cats in the village produced over 1000 prey items. A professor in America saw these figures and worked out that on this basis the cat population of Britain must be killing 100 million birds and small mammals each year! An article in the *Times* stated that 'Britain's wildlife may never have faced a more deadly onslaught.'

The mesmeric effect of big numbers seems to have stultified reason. It is not realistic just to multiply the number of catches of these rural cats by the entire cat population of Britain. Most cats are town cats with small ranges, and catch fewer items of prey than the village cats of this survey. The key question should have been this: are the numbers sustainable? The answer would seem to be yes.

While a quarter of Felmersham's house sparrows were consumed by the cats each year, after each breeding period the sparrow population doubled. In winter many householders feed garden birds, while nestboxes, garden trees and domestic buildings provide additional nesting sites, and in this way the bird population in villages and towns is kept at well above 'natural' levels. Even if there are a lot of cats in built-up areas, there are also a lot of birds. So the survey found that the house cat is a significant predator, and not that it is devastating Britain's bird population. The same, unfortunately, could not be said for birds everywhere. On continents cats rarely have a harmful effect on overall bird populations, but on small islands they can be disastrous.

British cats catch mice and other rodents more than birds. Despite some people's fears, the size of the country prevents these cats from making serious inroads into the bird population. On small islands, however, the story is unfortunately different.

Left *The ship's cat on Captain Scott's expedition to the South Pole in 1912, lying in his hammock. Sadly, he was swept overboard during a gale and never seen again.*

Old sea cats

Since the cat is so adaptable, it is not surprising that it has populated most corners of the globe. During the centuries after its emergence from Egypt the desire for trade and exploration took mankind all over the world; the rodent-catching cat travelled with them as an invaluable member of the ship's crew, and often stayed to found new cat colonies.

Captain James Cook, the most respected marine explorer of the eighteenth century, recorded in his journal that this novelty from the animal kingdom intrigued some of those now seeing it for the first time. On the Pacific island of Tonga the inhabitants 'were very fond of our cats of which they stole, for which two or three of them were flogged on board the *Discovery* more than once'. At Tahiti he noted that cats from a Spanish ship that had called there three years earlier, in 1774, had 'already turn'd wild and retir'd to the mountains'.

Opposite *The feral descendants of the cats that lived on former sub-Antarctic whaling and sealing stations continue to survive today: this one is on Marion Island.*

86

THE WILD SIDE OF CATS

The explorer Edward Wilson was one of those who perished on Captain Scott's ill-fated journey to the South Pole in 1912. The ship's cat was the first of his species to land and overwinter in Antarctica, and Wilson's diary reveals the kind attention that their companion received from the crew: 'He has a hammock of his own with the "hands" under the fo'c's'le. A real man o' war hammock with small blankets and a small pillow and the blankets over him. He has learned to jump into his hammock and creeps in under the blankets with his head on the tiny pillow.'

Sub-Antarctic cat colonies

Cats travelling on ships arrived at isolated islands all round the world; sometimes they were introduced to control rodents, but usually it was more accidental. In the days before factory ships, on sub-Antarctic islands used as bases for whaling and sealing, cats were often part of semi-permanent encampments. Even in such a harsh climate their feral descendants still flourish. On some islands they eat penguins, although these may have been found dead and scavenged; their usual prey consists of introduced rabbits or rats.

A helicopter survey of the cats of Courbet, in the tiny Kerguelen Islands in the southern Indian Ocean, found thirty-six that were all black or black and white; only one, a tabby that hung around the base station, was different. This similarity of colouring demonstrates what is called the 'founder effect' in a population that has developed from a very small number of marooned cats. By contrast the much larger island of Tasmania boasts a wide range of coat colours among the feral cat population.

The impact on island birds

Cats on islands take proportionally far more birds in their diet than do those on continents; the toll is especially heavy on species that spend much of their time on the ground. On sub-Antarctic islands the diving petrels are the most vulnerable, as they are a perfect recipe for cat success. They are only eight inches long and lay their single egg in accessible burrows in soft soil; in addition their incubation and fledging periods are unusually long.

On one island at the end of the nineteenth century just one cat was responsible for the extinction of an entire species, which happened to be the only flightless perching bird ever recorded. Stephens Island in New Zealand, only one square mile in area, was home to the Stephens Island Wren, found nowhere else on earth.

The bird was both discovered and made extinct by the lighthouse keeper's cat, which took its catches back home. The keeper, not recognising the bird, gave the bodies to an ornithologist. But before the wren's importance had been discovered the cat had worked its way through the small population of birds; they stood little chance because, apart from being flightless, they were nocturnal like the cat. As the New Zealand *Canterbury Press* reported in 1895: 'This is probably a record performance in the way of extermination. The English scientific world will hear simultaneously of its discovery and its disappearance.' Today all that remains are the skins of a few birds salvaged from the cat.

The Galapagos Islands cats

At the other end of the climatic spectrum from the sub-Antarctic islands are the equatorial Galapagos Islands in the Pacific, which offer an incredible demonstration of cats' ability to survive. The absence of fresh water on the islands should be fatal for them, but they prevent dehydration by catching grasshoppers, which contain a fair amount of liquid for their size; and the Galapagos cats shelter in crevices during the intense heat of midday. They are known to be resident on only five of the fourteen main islands, but four of these are the largest.

The Galapagos have a particularly significant range of native reptiles, but also a number of introduced feral animals. In addition to cats these include goats, pigs, cattle and dogs and they have had a harmful effect on the native species.

Among the special reptiles are the marine iguana, the only marine lizard in existence; unfortunately, young and hatching iguanas form a major item of prey for the cats. And natural conditions sometimes seem to conspire with the cats against the iguanas' continued survival. Two major ocean currents meet at the Galapagos, but about once every decade the warm El Niño current displaces the cold Humboldt and the hotter temperatures dramatically deplete the seaweeds on which the marine iguanas feed. In 1983 the conditions were the worst this century; on those islands without cats the iguana populations weathered the storm, but on the rest the extra pressure on the young was nearly final.

Parts of the islands are covered in volcanic lava so razor-sharp that even feral dogs and tortoises cannot cross them – yet the cat does. That makes it a threat to the unique Galapagos flightless cormorant, which is normally out of range of the feral animals. This bird nests in just one area, fishing in a particularly cold channel where it competes with another remarkable bird – the only penguin on the Equator! Shorn of wings, the cormorant

Australia has marsupial cats that evolved quite independently of the placental mammal cats found elsewhere in the world. The spotted-tailed native cat (Dasyurus maculatus) and other native cats are losing out as a result of competition from European shorthaired cats like the blotched tabby and habitat changes caused by farming.

has an advantage underwater, but on land that feature
has become a distinct drawback now that cats have been
introduced to the islands.

Cats in Australia

The First Fleet arrived from Britain in 1788, transporting
convicts rather than settlers. So the first British cats to
land were ships' cats like Trim, who accompanied the
navigator Matthew Flinders charting Australia's coasts.
When settlers arrived with cats they also brought the
rabbit. By the 1880s that had become a pest, and

A robust Australian feral cat: a blotched tabby with an old-style longhaired coat that does not tangle despite receiving no attention from man. This cat has become used to people as a result of hand-outs, yet keeps to a safe vantage point on unused farm machinery near some old buildings and eucalyptus trees.

thousands of cats were released on to farmland in a misguided attempt at control.

On mainland continents cats do not seem to be threatening wildlife populations, but the exception is Australia. Its 50 million years' isolation developed a special fauna of marsupials. In bush areas native species are in the introduced feral cat's diet, but fortunately the main prey is the introduced rabbit. Australia is also different from Europe and America in that its abundant small reptiles are easy prey for feral cats. There is a fierce split of opinion in Australia over cats and their threat to native wildlife, which has led to a 'cat curfew' in the state of Victoria.

Intriguingly, an examination of Aboriginal words for cat has led to the idea that some cats may have arrived ahead of Europeans, on Indonesian vessels.

The great survivor

The cat may be the supreme mammalian hunter, but it is also a most enterprising scavenger, ever ready to exploit a hand-out. When food is abundant its home range shrinks and more cats can be supported. The cat population adjusts to whatever level of food is available, which predisposes the animal to thrive in urban conditions. So when it emerged into the newly developing towns of Ancient Egypt its survival was assured: it was destined to become the most abundant cat species that has ever existed.

The Breeds

When is a breed not a breed? This Blue-cream is a variety of the Persian (Longhair) breed. Early this century its colour was thought of as an avoidable mistake, but it is now sought after. Yet in America colour patches in it are liked, while frowned upon in Britain. There is no overall international consensus of what makes a particular breed or variety – only the classifications from a series of registering bodies. So what makes a breed? Realistically, if a group of people recognise a type of cat as being distinct enough from others, then it is a breed. Yet there is no consistent biological criterion, and some modern 'breeds' are based on dubious or trivial distinctions. In contrast there are historic breeds that have been formed by geographical separation, like the Siamese, Korat and Angora: these are the most authentically distinct of true breeds.

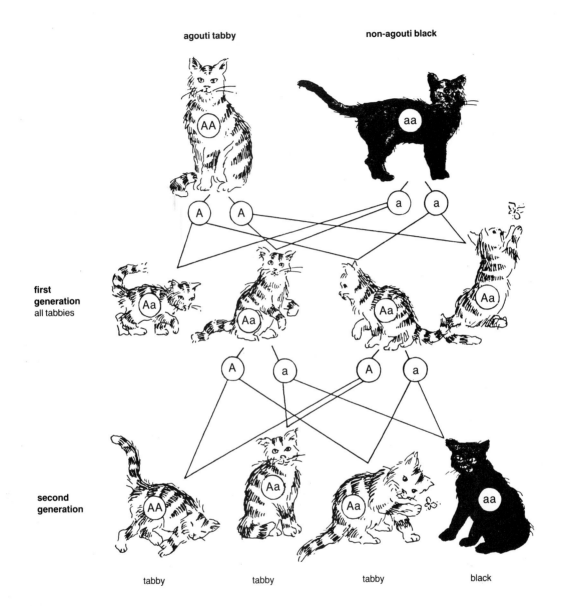

agouti tabby

non-agouti black

first generation
all tabbies

second generation

tabby   tabby   tabby   black

Where did the black cat go?
It's all to do with dominant
and recessive genes (see text).

5 The Original Tabby in All Its Guises

Genes, mutations and the ghost of a tabby

The basic cat is a tabby – although it is not a breed as such – and all cats would still look the same as the wild-type, fine-striped tabby if it were not for mutation. Thanks to horror movies this term is loaded with fear, yet it need not be so.

Genes determine the characteristics of the cat – eye colour, coat colour and length, and so on – and are inherited in pairs, one from each parent. The genes are borne on chromosomes, like beads on a necklace. Genes for each physical characteristic of the cat occur at definite points along this 'necklace'. These are normally duplicated exactly, to be passed on to the offspring. On extremely rare occasions, however, there will be a small flaw in the duplication and a mutated gene (known as a mutant allele) results. This can be passed on to subsequent generations. While mutation can result in deformities, it can also produce desirable changes: the wide range of coat colours and lengths in domestic cats – from the black cat to the Angora – arose as mutations.

However, there is more to the genetics of cat coat colours than meets the eye from just looking at the animal. In the tabby, where the coat is flecked (known as agouti) the hairs are banded with yellow; in the black parts of the tabby coat the yellow bands are missing (non-agouti). If

A young, beautifully marked agouti cat in the streets of Bangkok responds to a passing dog with the classic posture of fear/aggression: arched back, hair standing on end, legs stiffened to gain extra height, and a side-on approach to the enemy to give the impression of greater size.

tabby cats mated together only ever produce tabby kittens, both parents have identical agouti alleles which they pass on. Similarly, if black cats only ever produce black kittens, both parents have the same mutant allele.

But cross one of these tabbies with one of the black cats and they will only have tabby kittens. What has happened? Has the black disappeared? No, for if these tabby kittens are mated together when they become adult, black kittens will appear alongside tabby ones.

Generally one coat colour is dominant over another, which is recessive. The tabby's agouti gene is dominant to the non-agouti one (in this case black, but it could be any self, or single, colour). As a result a kitten that inherits a pair of agouti genes will be tabby; a kitten that receives one dominant (agouti) and one recessive (black) gene will also be tabby; but a kitten with two recessive black alleles will have a black coat. Most cat coat colour inheritance works in this simple manner of relative dominance.

Whatever a cat looks like, whether a Russian Blue or a Smoke Persian, it is genetically tabby. Every cat has tabby alleles. Even selfs are really tabby, despite the evidence of your own eyes. All that has happened is that the non-agouti allele has removed the paler area of the tabby pattern; the 'ghost' of a tabby pattern still shows in a certain light. Yet which tabby? For there are three types of tabby alleles: the wild-type, narrow-banded 'mackerel', the broader blotched tabby and the Abyssinian pattern.

The British Imperial Cat –
the blotched tabby

The geneticist Neil Todd traced the probable origins of the blotched tabby to medieval England; but did this mutation happen in England? Sixteenth-century Last

THE BREEDS

Supper paintings by Veronese and Bernardino Luini are among the first to show a blotched tabby. From the beginning of the same century comes the earliest representation I have seen, a marquetry panel by Fra Raffaele da Brescia. All three are by north Italian artists, so it may be in this part of Europe that the mutation occurred, subsequently travelling to England through trade via the great rivers of France which linked London and the English Channel with the Mediterranean. Working back from the present-day distribution of the mutation, it probably occurred around 1200.

I have dubbed the humble blotched tabby the British Imperial Cat, since it spread around the world in the wake of British colonialisation. In Britain, as the centuries passed the proportion of blotched tabbies in the cat population increased. The initial waves of British settlers sailing to America in the seventeenth century, Canada in the eighteenth and Australia in the nineteenth took with them cats that reflected the proportion of blotched tabbies in Britain at the time. The same proportions can still be seen today, for the blotched tabby became established in these colonised countries which had no existing domestic cat. In countries without British settlement, such as Egypt and Thailand, the numbers of blotched tabbies are minimal.

The blotched tabby thrives in urban conditions. That may be because it is less timid than the mackerel tabby, but its colouring may also be partly accountable for its success. While the mackerel tabby has open countryside camouflage, enabling it to lurk unnoticed in grassland, the black splodges of the blotched tabby blend well into urban jungle twilight; the low light conditions of northern woodlands and sub-Antarctic islands also favour the blotched markings.

Possibly the earliest representation of a blotched tabby: an early sixteenth-century marquetry panel from the Monastery of Monte Oliveto Maggiore, Siena, by Fra Raffaele da Brescia.

THE BREEDS

The Abyssinian – the full agouti tabby

A breed form of an agouti cat, the Abyssinian was recognised in 1882 and is one of the most distinctive breeds in the show cat world. It is a tabby with markings restricted to the head, legs and tail, and with an agouti body. But where is it from? Claims that it was a royal cat of Ancient Egypt are not based on hard evidence, but its name encourages belief, although Harrison Weir also recorded it as 'Russian' and 'Spanish'.

The Abyssinian is a breed form of the agouti cat, with tabby markings only on the head and tail. The tabby is not a breed, yet it is the antecedent of them all. In many breeds a tabby is a variety, while particular tabby markings are the basis for breeds like the Abyssinian, Egyptian Mau and Oriental Spotted Tabby.

The striped or mackerel tabby was so called because the pattern on its coat resembled the markings on a mackerel skin. In the USA it is often called a tiger pattern.

The Gayer-Anderson bronze cat shows head markings stylised into a scarab and tabby rings on the end of the tail. Could this be an Abyssinian?

Harrison Weir's drawing of a spotted tabby – probably a modified mackerel coat rather than a mutation.

The first one was brought to England by Captain Barrett Lennard in 1868 following a British military expedition to Abyssinia (now known as Ethiopia). Those keen to demonstrate an Egyptian connection stress the similarity of Aby markings to those of the North African wild cat, although it is closer to the jungle cat.

Breeders eliminated the leg markings of early Abyssinians, but on the cross-breed Abyssinian it reappears. This original agouti pattern of the Abyssinian is found in Russia, giving credence to Harrison Weir's 'Russian' name, though agoutis are found mainly from India to Singapore and may therefore be a south-east Asian mutation. Yet, as the agouti is dotted around the world, are these relics of a much earlier population?

Among Egypt's cats a third are mackerel tabbies – double the number of spotted tabbies. The spotted tabby is less likely to be a mutation than a modified mackerel in which stripes break to spots, as cats often have both.

Consequently the spotted and agouti may also have been around since the dawning of domestication. In Ancient Egyptian art both mackerel and spotted cats are shown; and, unless it is just a stylised representation, so is the agouti. In Egyptian bronzes coat markings are not normally shown, yet in the world's most famous Ancient Egyptian cat bronze, the Gayer-Anderson cat in the British Museum, the head markings are stylised into a scarab and the end of the tail has clear tabby rings. This could be a realistic representation of an Abyssinian.

6 The Moggie Shorthairs

Tough lives produce tough cats

Cats' coats divide into two main types, shorthair and longhair. Towards the end of the nineteenth century, when the cat fancy was established, native British and European Shorthairs ruled the roost. 'A high-class short-haired cat is one of the most perfect animals ever created,' said the standard-bearer of cat appreciation, Harrison Weir. But soon Longhairs took over, and even now many people overlook these Shorthairs and regard them as 'just house cats' rather than as breeds in their own right.

It was these shorthaired cats that spread through Europe with Roman trade, were burnt as witches' cats, lived around farmyards and even reached the Antarctic. The archetypal cat is the good old moggie tabby, be it brown, ginger or elegant silver. Centuries of living rough, alongside man, have produced a strong, hardy, streetwise animal. The build of these well-rounded cats is referred to as 'cobby'.

The moggie reaches America

A ginger and white shorthaired moggie – tough, disease-resistant and streetwise.

There were probably cats on board the ships of Columbus's first voyage to the New World, in 1492; from a letter written in 1495 it is known for certain that they were taken there on his second voyage, in 1493–5. Spanish settlement of southern North America, and British and French settlement to the north, suggest that there were originally two main populations of domestic cat. Remarkably, this is borne out by the genetics of the cats today. Investigations into the genetic profiles of these cat populations across the range of coat colours and lengths show that the cats of Philadelphia, Boston and New York, for instance, are more English in origin, while those in Mexico City, San Francisco and Dallas have Spanish ancestry.

When these shorthaired cats reached America in the company of emigrants, they had a rugged life there too. The hand-to-mouth existence of the early pioneers, combined with battles between settlers and with native Americans, ensured that many cats were abandoned to a feral life.

Snobbery versus sense

When the fancy was introduced in the USA snobbery dictated that English-born cats were breed cats, while native-bred ones were 'just cats'. As a result the first Shorthair to be registered by the CFA was a British ginger tom, in 1900. But fortunately American common sense prevailed and soon cats that fitted the standard, despite unrecorded lineage, were also registered. The first true American cat to be enrolled was Buster Brown, in 1904.

After the devastation of World War II there were few pedigree stud animals left in Europe. Pedigrees are only records of lines of good-type cats, and if there are too few of these animals available it makes sense to look for good cats of the right type in their area of origin so as to widen the genetic base. To augment the numbers of the heavy-

The modern British Shorthair breed has been changed from the rugged lines of the natural house and alley cat in Britain by crossing with Persians, giving a more rounded head.

built British Shorthair, breeders should have chosen from house cats and farm cats. Instead, matings were made to far slimmer foreign body Shorthairs, and unsurprisingly the massive build disappeared. To reintroduce it, breeders crossed their cats with solidly built Persians. Why? Was it the snob value of a piece of paper that said an animal had a pedigree?

The result was a different animal – with a softer coat, a broader, Persian head, and the straight nose changed to a more Persian beak. Since then, American cat breeding associations have recognised the British Shorthair as a distinct breed.

However, American breeders themselves were not immune to trying crosses with Persians. The same physical changes occurred, producing an animal that many people liked; but it wasn't an honest-to-goodness American Shorthair, and there was rebellion among US cat fanciers. A standard was drawn up for the new cats, which were now dubbed Exotic Shorthairs; at the same time a rapid search was made to find unaffected lines of the American Shorthair, and non-pedigree cats were registered. As a result, the most true-to-type pedigree cat deriving from the shorthaired British house cat is, ironically, nowadays to be found in America.

7 Longhairs of the West and Middle East

Early confusion and muddled breeding

Harrison Weir's drawing of his 'ideal' longhaired cat shape. Regrettably, his guidelines were taken too literally by breeders and the Angora was replaced by the Persian.

The basic, wild-type cat is shorthaired; longhaired cats are probably the result of a genetic mutation (see p. 97). Longhairs have flourished for centuries in mountainous and northern regions where the rigours of the climate make thick fur an essential for survival, and in their natural, 'unbred' state these cats' coats remain unmatted without grooming – a functional covering, not one that has been reduced to a fashion accessory.

Among European cat fanciers, in the nineteenth century different longhairs tended to be treated in somewhat cavalier fashion as a single breed. Harrison Weir himself distinguished between the Angora, the Persian, the Maine Coon and the Russian, but noted sadly in 1891: 'I am fully aware that many cross-bred cats are sold as Russian, Angoran and Persian.'

He described what he felt was the right head shape for longhairs: 'Head: round and broad across and between the eyes, of medium size; nose rather short; ears ordinary size, but looking small, being surrounded with long hair.' Breeders interpreted Weir's standard over-literally; combined with the fact that most judging was done on the basis of colour only, this approach to breeding sealed the fate of the different builds of longhair. The long, graceful shape of the Angora disappeared when it was bred with

the heavier Persian, and was not seen again in the West until the 1950s when new animals were brought from Turkey.

Meanwhile the Persian itself suffered as judges and breeders seized eagerly on that phrase 'nose rather short'; comparing pictures of Persians exhibited at the early cat shows with those of the present day confirms how the nose has shrunk. This led to the Peke-faced Persian. Is this the ultimate creation in cat breeding, or a frightful distortion of what a cat should look like? Fortunately in recent years new breeds of Longhair have been recognised, including ironically the Turkish Angora, the oldest natural longhair. Cats of original physical conformation are now quite literally in a class of their own.

The Angora

When Turkey became a republic in 1923, after the collapse of the Ottoman Empire, the ancient fortified hilltop village of Angora became the new capital of Ankara. Yet even today the old village remains intact, protected from urbanisation by its steep approaches; the village women can still be seen beating the thick goat and sheep fleeces for which the place is famous. And it is a particular pleasure to see true Angora longhair cats, with their classic, elegant build, aquiline nose and narrow head, living as feral and house cats in their original setting.

After Western breeders' systematic elimination of slim-build longhairs, today it is a joy to see feral Angoras with fine, unaffected noses in the old hill town of Angora in Ankara, Turkey.

THE BREEDS

Opposite *In the seventeenth and eighteenth centuries the elegance of the longhaired cats made them a desirable status symbol for the French aristocracy, who lavished attention on them. Jean-Baptiste Perronneau,* Girl with a Cat, *1745. This cat still clearly has the true shape of an Angora.*

Left *By the nineteenth century many cats had become well-loved household pets. Louis Léopold Boilly,* Gabrielle Arnault, *1813.*

These cats have a range of colours and patterns, for it is the length and type of coat and the build of the animal which distinguishes an Angora, not its colour. Yet it was white Angoras which became the darlings of the wealthy during the six hundred years of the Ottoman Empire; and they achieved the same modish status in Europe – mainly in France – after their introduction by Venetian traders in the late Middle Ages, or even earlier with the returning crusaders.

French attitudes to the cat remained ambivalent for a long time. While superstition and persecution were the lot of the common cat, the longhairs' good looks ensured their acceptance in the highest social circles. The power behind the throne during the reign of Louis XIII, Cardinal Richelieu (1585–1642), left pensions to his fourteen cats, at least one of which was a '*chatte angora*'. Seventeenth-century ladies of fashion lavished attention on their pets: Antoinette du Ligier de la Garde Deshoulières, 'Tenth Muse' at Louis XIV's court, wrote poetic love letters from her cat to the one owned by the Duchess of Béthune. Yet to placate his people the King was still lighting bonfires on which cats were ritually burnt (see p. 51).

A contemporary depiction of the original 'Persian': a grey smoke Angora-type cat with full plumed tail, sitting between a young Persian prince and his teacher. This miniature of about 1675 comes from Isfahan and has been attributed to Ali Quli Jabbadar. Since Moslem art has a bias towards calligraphy, images of cats in Persian art are remarkably few; nevertheless cats have been accepted in Moslem society for far longer than in the West.

The Turkish Van

Turkey is also noted for another longhaired cat, although the Turkish Van bred and shown in Britain would not be recognised as such in its homeland, the Lake Van region of Anatolia. I travelled there expecting to find that the local cats were white Angoras with characteristic auburn patches on the head and around each ear, and that their tails would be, as stated in the official standard of the Governing Council of the Cat Fancy (GCCF), 'full, medium length, auburn in colour'. But I arrived in the

Turkish families sometimes take their cats with them when they have picnics by Lake Van.

The adult cat here is of the single-colour type recognised locally as the true Van cat,

while the kitten, with its auburn patches, is of the type recognised in Britain.

town of Van to find that the true Van cat was a charming, delicate, all-white Angora; hardly any of the cats I saw had the markings that I had thought were the Van's distinctive feature.

I discussed this with many local people, including Professor Gure of Van University, who has made a special study of them; everyone affirmed that a Van cat is all-white. For the local people, what distinguishes a Van is its odd eyes, preferably one green and one blue, although yellow and blue are also acceptable; such odd-eyed cats are selected from litters. The cats from Ankara, they say, have both eyes blue.

Why this misunderstanding over the identity of the Van? Up until recently, mountainous Anatolia remained isolated and its cats were unknown to the rest of the world. In 1955, two cat lovers travelling in the area brought back to Britain a pair of auburn-marked cats; it is from these that the West's line developed. But the townspeople told me that they were definitely not proper Van cats. Nowadays Anatolia is accessible to tourists, which has led to the unfortunate theft by them of a number of these highly prized cats.

In Britain the Van is known as the swimming cat. Various owners in the town said that their cats accompanied them on picnics beside the lake, played in the shallows and were strong swimmers. Despite cats' general dislike of water, this kind of behaviour is not unusual in the Eastern Mediterranean. The shorthaired, slim-built cats of the Greek and Turkish coasts regularly jump from moored boats and swim to land and back. Remarkably, the longhaired Van's coat dries unmatted.

The Van cat is often called the swimming cat, and its fur, despite its length, dries unmatted. Here one enters the water of Lake Van. However this behaviour is not unusual in the Eastern Mediterranean, where cats of all kinds often swim to land from moored boats and back again.

Persians – natural breed or invented?

Does the Persian cat come from Persia? Some say yes, others no. The distinctive features of the Angora had, as already mentioned, been swamped by the early part of this century. Britain's GCCF then decided to call all longhaired cats Longhairs, while in the United States they were dubbed Persians. Today's Persian has a full 'powder puff' coat, while that of the reintroduced Angora is much lanker. These Persians could never survive an uncombed life on the street; with their changed head and coat, they are an 'invention' of breeding.

Yet before Western breeders imposed these differences, were the longhaired cats of Turkey and Persia identified as different from each other? Longhair cats of Angoran form are found from Istanbul to north-east Iran, beyond the Caspian Sea; these are distinct from the heavier-coated cats to the north (see p. 127–9).

The eighteenth-century French naturalist the Comte de Buffon quoted the sixteenth-century Italian traveller Pietro della Valle, who is often erroneously credited with introducing the longhaired cat to Europe:

'In Europe . . . there is a species of cats which properly belong to the province of Chorazan [in the north-east of Iran, between the USSR and Afghanistan]. Their beauty consists in the colour of their hair, which is grey, and uniformly the same over the whole body, except that it is darker on the back and head, and clearer on the breast and belly, where it approaches to whiteness. Besides, the hair is fine, shining, soft as silk, and so long, that, though not frizzled, it forms ringlets in some parts, and particularly under the throat. The most beautiful part of the body is the tail, which is very long, and covered with hair five or six inches in length. They extend and turn it upon their back, like the squirrel, the point resembling a plume of feath-

The modern bred Persian, with its thick, full coat, could never survive without constant grooming by its owner.

ers. They are very tame; and the Portuguese have brought them from Persia into India.' From this description it appears, that the Persian cats resemble, in colour, those we call Chartreux cats [an old breed of French grey cats], and that, except in colour, have a perfect resemblance to the cat of Angora.

Buffon had not seen the 'Persian' cats himself, but was familiar with the Angora in France. His last sentence reveals his belief that there was no difference between an Angora and a Persian except in colour – that in build and appearance they were the same. This Persian was a grey

123

CAT of ANGORA

A Bell Sculp.t

'Cat of Angora', from the Comte de Buffon's Histoire Naturelle of 1756. Buffon noted that the only difference then between the Angora and cats from Persia was their colour.

smoke form of the Angora, and luckily a contemporary picture exists.

The state cat of Maine

Maine, New England, is home to one of the most rugged individualists of the cat world, the Maine Coon. The oldest indigenous breed of the United States has the distinction of being the state cat of Maine. Its unfortunate name was given by early frontiersmen, who thought it resulted from the implausible breeding of a domestic cat with a raccoon. It is a large animal with a magnificent shaggy coat, which helped it survive New England's harsh winters as a semi-feral farm cat.

The longhair gene is likely to have arrived with immigrant cats on ships, and the most romantic story of the breed's origin involved the ill-fated Queen Marie Antoinette, who owned six Angoras. During the French Revolution a plot was hatched for the royal family to escape from France on the ship *Sally*, whose captain was a man named Samuel Clough from Wiscasset, Maine. The plan failed, but the captain sailed with the household effects – including the six cats. Outdoor life in New England would have turned the courtly Angora into the all-American Maine Coon.

An alternative theory, based on interpretations of coat colour distributions, holds that the cat arrived with the Vikings from Scandinavia. A Viking settlement has been excavated in Newfoundland, and a Norse coin from the reign of Olav the Kyrre (1067–93) was found in Maine. In Iceland in 1200 one adult tomcat skin was worth three fox skins, and so was a trading asset. Some of these cats could have been taken to America from the Iceland or Greenland staging posts. A localised feral population

could have persisted until it integrated with settlers' cats centuries later. Supporting this, the Maine cat closely resembles the Norwegian Forest cat or Norsk Skaukatt (see p. 128).

In the early days of cat showing in America the Maine Coon reigned supreme: at the Madison Square Garden show in 1895 a Maine cat was best of show. But the arrival of fashionable pedigree Persians forced them to retire to the ranks of the farming community for many decades. Then in 1953 a club was started at Skowhegan, Maine, and in 1976 the CFA bestowed championship status back on to America's finest. As with the Shorthair (see p. 108), common sense had at last overcome snobbery.

Above *The Maine Coon developed as a robust farm cat well suited to the outdoor life in New England. However, as breeders' cats and more house cats in the USA are kept for their whole lives indoors, perversely a new generation of Maine Coons is intimidated by the outside world.*

The Norwegian Forest cat and the return of the Russian

Below After the early cat shows the Russian longhaired cat was forgotten in the West until 1991 when, now called the Siberian, it made a comeback at the International Cat Show in New York.

The Norsk Skaukatt of Norway also lives as a feral and farm cat. It is probable that the longhair gene travelled from Asia Minor by Viking and river trade routes north through Russia. Ancient Norse legends about a cat with a long bushy tail hint at a long association with the region.

In Britain, Russian longhairs were displayed at the

The Norwegian Forest is probably the cat with a long bushy tail that appears in old Norse legends. All northern longhairs have a coat that is thick and warm but also sheds water and snow easily.

early cat shows. One of these cats was owned by Harrison Weir, who characterised its appearance in these words: 'The mane was very large, long and dense, a woolly texture, with coarse hairs among it; colour was of dark tabby. The eyes large and prominent, . . . the ears large by comparison with small tufts full of long, woolly hair, . . . the tail thickly covered with hair the same length from the base to the tip.' This description could well apply to today's Norwegian Forest cat.

The development of these robust cats was formed by the same harsh climatic conditions. All these northern longhairs have a woolly undercoat, through which grows a coarser hair that sheds water and snow. The longhair gene is particularly abundant among Russian cats, while Denmark and Sweden have near-identical versions, the Racekatte and the Rugkatt.

Pedigree breeding of the Norwegian Forest cat gained interest in Norway in the 1930s; it lapsed during World War II, but was revived in the 1970s. Due to lack of contact the Russian cat was forgotten in the West. Then, like a ghost from the past, at the 1991 International Cat Show in New York a true Russian cat was exhibited. It had been brought from the USSR by Olga Frolova, President of the Soviet Union's new cat fancy, and breeder David Boehm, who call it the Siberian.

Untangling the breeds

The longhair breeds are now recognised individually again. There are three types of coat: the Angora type, the northern cats and modern Persians.

8 The Cats of the Far East

The journey east from Egypt

The ancestors of the European cat travelled north and west by trade routes; the forebears of the cats of Asia went east in the same way. Arab and Indian coastal trade is of great antiquity, and a sure route to south-east Asia. In the past, Nile boat crews refused to sail if there was no cat on board, and even in the 1930s the writer and traveller Alan Villiers still found cats considered essential to deal with rats on board the traditional dhows in the Arabian and Red Seas.

The stability of the Roman Empire in the West and the Chinese Han Empire in the East enabled overland trade between the two to flourish from about 130 BC to AD 300. Camel trains from the trading centres of the Middle East set off regularly along the Silk Route which crossed Asia and led to China. But the 'barbarian expansion' of nomadic tribes from central Asia destroyed both empires, along with the trade route, for hundreds of years.

After evidence of cats in China around AD 400 there is a gap until they reappear around the year 1000, when the Silk Route was re-established. When these rare animals arrived the noble Chinese recipients chained the adults, a practice which prevailed for centuries and, when the cat spread further afield in the Far East, was also carried on in Japan. But these animals, though highly regarded,

At an isolated rural temple in Thailand this Buddhist abbot is surrounded by various cats including on the left a traditional Siamese, and on the right a tortoiseshell point. Nowadays breeders of Siamese are eager to produce litters with such unusual colourpoints – but it seems that cats often get there first, unaided.

were not just pets: in China they were used to guard silk-worm cocoons from rodents.

A silk scroll with the signature and seals of the Ming Emperor Hsuan-tsung (1398–1435) shows kittens at play (pp. 142–3). Although this may well be genuine – the Emperor was an accomplished artist – it could also be an eighteenth-century copy. But either way it shows that by the 1700s at the latest white with orange, and white with black and orange (calico) cats were present in China; they would also reach Japan and other regions of south-east Asia.

The slim, 'foreign' build

While the build of typical, well-rounded British cats is described as 'cobby', as mentioned earlier, that of the slim shorthairs of south-east Asia is called 'foreign'. The reason for the difference is not certain. These hot and cool climate builds may have mutated after domestication; alternatively hybridisation with African wild cats in hot climates may have reinforced the slim build, while

Harrison Weir's drawing of 'the royal cat of Siam' shows the relatively slim, 'foreign' build of south-east Asian cats when they first arrived in nineteenth-century Britain, not the extreme shape of today's Western show cats.

matings in northern Europe with European forest cats could have imparted a heavier build there.

The Cat Book Poems

Ayutthaya was the capital of Siam (Thailand) from 1350 until it was destroyed in 1767 by the invading Burmese. During this period a series of Cat Book Poems was written and illustrated, covering all the known cats of Thailand. The poems show seventeen types of cats, most of which are black and white and can still be seen in that country around the wats or temples. This invaluable record depicts the Siamese, called the Vichien Mat in the poems, the Korat and the Copper. Significantly, there are no ginger, tortoiseshell or calico cats in its illustrations, yet today these are abundant in south-east Asia. The orange gene probably travelled via the Silk Route across Asia, while the original poem cats arrived earlier by sea trade.

The royal cat of Siam

When the Siamese was first exhibited in the West, at the inaugural Crystal Palace Cat Show of 1871, one shocked reaction was that it seemed 'an unnatural nightmare kind of cat'. But more cat lovers shared Harrison Weir's assessment: 'Among the beautiful varieties of the domestic cat brought into notice by the cat shows, none deserves more attention than "The Royal Cat of Siam".'

In the past these cats were restricted to the royal household and temples of Thailand. A Thai belief exists that, when a spiritually enlightened person dies, their spirit can enter a cat until the animal dies too. In the past, at the death of a Thai monarch his favourite cat was entombed with him, though a small hole was left in the roof; when the cat emerged from this hole it was believed to contain the king's spirit.

Royal cats were occasionally presented as diplomatic gifts, the most celebrated being the pair given to the British Consul General in 1884, which were brought to Britain. From contemporary sketches and photographs of these early arrivals it is clear that Western breeders have since imposed a more 'oriental' shape than the real Thai

A Korat cat by a farm building in Thailand, where in country areas it is believed to have power over the weather and to bring good fortune.

The Korat as depicted in the Thai Cat Book Poems.

cat possesses. 'Foreign' build is not accentuated in Thailand's pet Siamese and those living feral around Buddhist temples, and Thai breeders such as Major General Pengrpicha perpetuate the traditional build.

Siamese cats are frequently described as having different-coloured 'points' – the point of the face, the ears, legs and tail. The Siamese mutation causes reduced pigment production in the hair fibres on the hotter parts of the body. The cat's skin is cooler at the thinner areas – the points – and so more pigment is produced there.

The Korat

Another Thai breed, known for many centuries as the Si-Sawat, is beautifully described in the Cat Book Poems: 'The hairs are smooth, with roots like clouds and tips like silver. The eyes shine like dewdrops on a lotus leaf.' The modern name was given by King Rama V in the nineteenth century after he had enquired where these cats came from – Korat is a region in the east of the country.

135

Korats live feral throughout Thailand, but are no-where common. In the dry north-east and centre the rain cloud colour of this cat is believed to hold power over the weather. At the end of the dry season farmers hold an enthusiastic procession featuring a Korat cat, over which they pour water to induce rain for crop fertility. The cats' silvery sheen symbolises prosperity and good fortune, so they used to be given to new brides and people worthy of respect.

When Siamese cats were reaching Britain the Korat arrived too, but at the National Cat Club Show in 1896 the judges disregarded it as a 'blue rather than biscuit col-oured' Siamese. Only in 1959, when a pair of Korats went to the USA, did the Western cat world pay any attention. The Korat was accepted as a breed in the USA in 1966, but not in Britain until 1975 – it was thought to be too similar to the Russian Blue, which had been introduced from Archangel in northern Russia in the 1860s and had gained general acceptance. Like all 'blue' cats the Korat has genes for a black coat plus a 'dilution' gene which reduces the colour density to a soft grey. Today's main breeding centre is America, where breed societies have kept the Korat true to type, while in Bangkok interest in showing Korats is growing.

The Burmese

Another cat from the Thai Poems, the Thong Daeng or Copper, is the progenitor of today's Burmese, which itself was named and recreated in America. In the 1890s a Mr Young of Harrogate in Yorkshire imported one, which he described as a 'chocolate variety of royal Siamese cat . . . rich chocolate or seal, with darker face, ears and tail; the legs are a shade darker which intensifies towards the feet'. The darker colour was considered 'an accidental deviation' and forgotten outside south-east Asia until in 1930 Dr Thompson, a US Navy psychiatrist, took one home from Rangoon. It was crossed to a Siamese, and the kittens crossed back to the mother.

What emerged were three types of coat: normal Siamese; darker-bodied but still with points like the mother; and fully solid, dark chocolate brown. The last of these was the first Burmese. The dark brown (or sable) Burmese breed true, and a Burmese gene is recognised. Although new to the West the gene is widespread in south-east Asia, where Coppers and Burmese occur naturally. Siamese and Burmese genes interact unusually: they produce the halfway colour of Coppers by 'incomplete dominance' (see Tonkinese, p. 154).

In the early 1950s the Burmese cat reached Britain, where selection has been in favour of the slim build of modern show Siamese, whereas in America the Burmese has retained a robust body. A wide range of coat colours has developed, which seems perverse as the authentic feature of the breed is the original colour. There was much early inbreeding in the USA, which may have led to recent serious skull problems in one line.

At Chiang Mai in Thailand I met Professor Edward Rose, an American, and his Thai wife Malee, the leading cat breeders in that country. They have a fine Copper tom called Woot, which to quote Edward is giving the Burmese breed 'a genetic shot in the arm'. With Burmese queens Woot has sired Copper and Burmese kittens, some of which are now in the USA. Where the old breeds still exist in their regions of origin it is crazy not to return to them as a true conformation guide and to strengthen the genetic base, while not depleting numbers in these regions.

Right *Painting of a Copper from the Thai Cat Book Poems, and the new Burmese* (below), *with genetic input from Thai Coppers.*

138

The Birman – the sacred cat of Burma

While the Birman might be a French breeder's invention of the 1920s, the romance of the alternative is so strong that it is tempting to believe it. Among the forested hills of north-east Burma lay the subterranean temple of Lao-Tsun. The Birmans, long-haired cats with Siamese markings and white feet, were the temple's sacred cats. A British army officer, Major Russell Gordon, saw them there in 1885.

In the legend of their origin long ago a cat named Sinh was the oracle for a spiritually enlightened temple priest

The Birman sealpoint was first seen in Europe just after World War I. According to legend, the cat acquired its white feet when the soul of a dying priest passed through them into its body.

of the Kittah religion, Mun-Ha. As an army of invading Thais stood at the gates Mun-Ha died, and his cat jumped on to him. When his soul passed into the cat its feet whitened, purified by their contact. The other priests, encouraged by this transmutation, routed their enemies. Sinh refused all food and died seven days later, when Mun-Ha's soul was released from earth.

Two Birman cats were apparently sent to France in 1919, and from 1926 photographs and articles about the 'new' cats began to appear. Support for an Asian origin strengthened in 1960 when two cats from Tibet were found which were identical to Birmans. While the long coat may have occurred by mutation, the movement of Buddhist monks in the Himalayan region could have caused the meeting of the longhair gene and the Siamese coat pattern. The white socks caused by a white spotting gene are not unique: in early cat shows white socks were often seen on Siamese, and in Thailand I have seen many Siamese with white socks among pets and temple cats. As all the required features are in this broad region, it seems mean-minded not to accept the Birman as an Asian cat.

Foreign or Oriental shorthairs

The foreign build black and black and white cats of the Cat Poems are now overlooked as breeds in their own country. In the 1950s British breeders developed a solid chocolate brown of foreign build, followed by a white, lilac and at last black. Until 1991 these were known as 'Foreign' while in North America they were and still are 'Oriental', a term which in Britain applied only to patterned cats. Now in Britain all cats of Siamese-derived build are termed 'Oriental', leaving other slim breeds to be grouped as 'Foreign'.

Kinky tails and the princesses

When Siamese cats first arrived in Britain they often had a kinked tail, which was seen by many owners as a charming exotic feature. A late nineteenth-century standard of points went so far as to note that the Siamese was often distinguished by the kink in its tail. And in 1903 the Hon. Secretary of the Siamese Cat Club wrote that 'a knot or kink in the tail is a peculiarity of the breed, and therefore desirable . . . in Siam it is highly prized, and cats given by the King as presents of value to important people have had this distinction.'

Since it is a natural feature of the south-east Asian cat it is unfortunate that fashion went against it among breeders, who outlawed it as a serious fault; it seems even more regrettable now that in its homeland an emerging interest in cat showing is following the Western lead. Recent breeding selection in the West has promoted the different and freaky, so if kinky tails had entered the international scene later than they did they would probably now be considered a positive feature.

Britain's Manx cat (see p. 168) had only a local distribution, while the Asian or kinky tails have a massive distribution and in south-east Asia are the commonest type of cat. This disparity has been ignored by the Western centres of show breeding. Perversely, while the gene for a short tail can be lethal in the Manx, it is an encouraged breed, while the safe Asian kinked tail is regarded as a serious fault except in the Bobtail (see p. 148).

The kinky tail varies from a single bend to a complex spiral of angles caused by distorted vertebrae that are frequently fused, often giving a shortened, clubbed-ended tail. Some cats' tails are reduced in length from the standard twenty-two to seven vertebrae.

Following pages
Detail of a calico cat with a bird, from a silk scroll attributed to the fifteenth-century Ming Emperor Hsuan-tsung. Even if, as some scholars believe, this is a later copy, it still shows that by the eighteenth century cats with white, black and orange markings had reached China – probably overland via the Silk Route.

A Thai monk holding a Siamese kitten with a clear kink in its tail. This malformation, caused by distorted or missing vertebrae, is frequently encountered among these cats in their south-east Asian homeland but was outlawed by Western breeders. There is a historic bond between Buddhist monks and cats in Asia which has aided the distribution and survival of oriental cats.

The most beautiful explanation of the kinky tail is offered by an old Thai fable that the royal Siamese cat provided the kink as a safe place to hold the rings of princesses while they bathed. More realistically, the widespread nature of the kinky tails suggests a 'founder effect': if initially only a few cats reached the East by the sea route from Egypt and the Middle East, and the genetic trait appeared in one of these animals, it would have become widespread in the population. My survey of Thailand's cats revealed 60 per cent to have Asian kinky tails, while other surveys have shown that Hong Kong to the north has 30 per cent but western Malaysia to the south has 65 per cent and Singapore 70 per cent, suggesting that the kinky tail may have begun in the Malay peninsula.

Because of a Russian connection kinky tails are common in an American town. Alaska was once part of the Russian Empire. Before it was sold to the USA in 1867 its old capital, Sitka, had trading links with eastern Asia, through which kinky tails arrived.

The Japanese Bobtail

In the sixth century Buddhism reached Japan, followed by things Chinese, and Buddhist monks may have brought the cat. The traditional belief, however, is that it was the Japanese Emperor Ichijo, who ruled a thousand years ago, who introduced cats from China.

It was an opportune time to arrive, for during what was known as the Heian Period aesthetics were the essence of courtly life and the Emperor ennobled his own cat, Myobu-no-Omoto. Cats became the consorts of the nobility and were given the endearment name of *tama* or jewel. The attachment of court and cat was long-lived, for

Opposite *Hiroshige's
nineteenth-century woodblock
print of a Japanese Bobtail,*
Cat Looking at Fields at
Asakusa, *from* 100 Views of
Edo. *For many centuries cats
were synonymous with the
nobility in Japan. After 1603,*
*when Tokugawa seized power
as Shogun, he controlled the
nobles by requiring their
families to live as hostages at
Tokyo. At the same time the
aristocratic symbol of walking
a cat on a leash was banned.
Once released, cats became*
*widespread and Bobtails were
portrayed in many works
of art.*
Above *Echoes of Ancient
Egypt in modern Japan: the
interior of the Gotoku-ji
Beckoning Cat Temple in
Tokyo.*

until the seventeenth century the Japanese aristocracy kept their cats on leashes. The domestic cat so closely associated with the nobility was distrusted in folk tales, but once it got loose from the leash its numbers and familiarity grew. Japan's long period of isolationism prevented it becoming colonised by Western imperialist powers – and by the blotched tabby.

Asian tail is seen at its most reduced in the Japanese Bobtail, and the tail bones often curve round, making it seem even shorter. That Bobtails had become common by the early nineteenth century is shown by Kuniyoshi's sketches of cats from roadside way-stations.

In Japan many cats were predominantly white, often with mackerel tabby. Most famous are the queens with a mainly white calico form of tortoiseshell – tricolours, known in Japan as *mi-ke*, and usually bobtailed. In Tokyo I met robust white and black bobtail males, fathers of litters containing *mi-ke* females and bicolour males – all bobtailed. Watching them play was to see Kuniyoshi's sketches come to life.

The Japanese Bobtail cat became taken for granted, and it took World War II for both Japan and the rest of the world even to begin to realise that here was an ancient breed of cat. The occupying American forces introduced cat shows – but although the Japanese showed interest in the other breeds they ignored the Bobtail. Then in 1968 several of these animals were taken to the USA and became recognised by North American cat fancy organisations and the CFA in Japan; the Bobtail has, however, yet, to conquer Britain and Europe.

Echoes of Bubastis

In Tokyo white statue cats with a raised paw are for sale, and are often put on shop counters for good fortune. They are primarily bought to place as offerings at the Gotoku-ji Beckoning Cat Temple. Alongside the temple small beckoning cat prayer boards for lost or sick cats are hung up. On my visits there I was met by a number of very welcoming cats, and the welcome of such a cat in the past is said to have saved a passing feudal lord. Intrigued, he followed the cat into the temple; a thunderbolt then crashed to earth where the nobleman had been standing. Consequently the cat was seen as an incarnation of the goddess of mercy.

Inside the temple are ranks of cat statues upon the altar; black- and saffron-robed Buddhist monks intone texts while striking resonant gongs and drums. The ashes of cremated cats used to be interred below a shrine to the original cat. Although the cat is not being worshipped as such, there is in this serene place a strong echo of ancient Bubastis.

*A red point Himalayan,
descendant of a Siamese-
marked Persian-build cat first
bred from in 1947.*

9 New Breeds

Self-portrait of Harrison Weir (1824–1905), cat illustrator, Father of the Cat Fancy and author of Our Cats, and All about Them. *He was also an authority on poultry breeding and a judge at poultry and pigeon shows. This combination of experience formed the ideal background when he became the pioneer of cat showing and breeding – his purpose in setting up shows was to gain wider public appreciation of the cat.*

Harrison Weir and the first cat show

No one person has had as much effect on the lives of domestic cats as Harrison Weir. He recognised that the cat had suffered, in his words, 'long ages of neglect, ill-treatment and absolute cruelty', and so he started to organise cat shows

. . . that different breeds, colour, markings might be more carefully attended to, and the domestic cat would then possess a beauty and attractiveness to its owner unobserved and unknown because uncultivated before.

I hoped that by these shows the too often despised cat will meet with the attention and kind treatment that every dumb animal ought to receive at the hands of humanity.

He devised schedules for the first show, which was held at Crystal Palace in London on 13 July 1871 and caught the popular imagination. Weir's 'Points of Excellence', the standards for judging at the first show, became the basis for all subsequent shows, including in 1895 America's first official show at New York's Madison Square Garden.

The National Cat Club that started in 1887 was the first registering body; keeping central records established animals' pedigrees. In 1910 registration was ceded to the newly formed Governing Council of the Cat Fancy. In

North America the Cat Fanciers' Association is the leading body, but there are also a number of others.

New outlook

Specialist clubs for breeds started in 1900 with the Silver Society for the new Chinchilla Persians, followed by the Blue Persian Society in 1901. The greater competition and interest that the clubs encouraged 'sharpened up' the cats, as typified by the Blue Persians. Early Blues' eyes were likely to be green, but by 1900 cats without the desired orange eyes would not win. A few white hairs

Judging in the ring at one of the early Crystal Palace cat shows.

became disastrous for showing, while formerly a white throat patch had been no disadvantage.

The Siamese became the main show shorthair, and in the USA it became the most popular pedigree pet: 4 million were owned, twice as many as the number of Persians. The development of breeds from the Siamese demonstrates the pattern of breeding this century, by crossing and mutation selection.

The Himalayan (Colourpoint Longhair)

In Britain in 1947 a Siamese-marked Persian-build cat of unknown ancestry was incorporated into a breeding programme of Siamese/Persian matings, and the descriptively named Colourpoint Longhair was born. Breeding interest in North America in the 1950s produced the romantically named Himalayans.

The Balinese

This breed is Siamese with long hair, caused by a recessive mutation. Before the 1950s the occasional longhairs in Siamese litters were put down as freaks. The Balinese was recognised for championship status in the USA in 1970.

Changing colourpoints

The colouring of the original Siamese imported to the West was termed by breeders 'sealpoint'. Hidden among its gene package were recessive and dilute genes, which gave the additional 'classic' colours of blue and chocolate points; these in turn gave lilac. The newer colours, such as red, were produced by outcrossing to non-Siamese – in this case to a red tabby; these are recognised as types of Siamese in Britain, but not in America, where they are called Colourpoint Shorthairs. Yet I have found tabby and tortie point Siamese among Thai temple cats. Left to their own devices, cats often get there first.

The Tonkinese

This is a new name for an old breed that was reinvented. The Tonkinese was produced in Canada in the 1960s as a cross between Siamese and Burmese, with halfway

Opposite *The Balinese is a longhaired Siamese. Formerly regarded as freaks and destroyed, they are now highly esteemed .*

Above *Concealed among the genes of the sealpoint Siamese when brought to the West were recessive and dilute genes, from which the other 'classic' colours of chocolate, blue and* lilac emerged. This is a chocolate point, not at first well received by many breeders, being described as a 'poor seal'.

colouring, the same as south-east Asia's Coppers. This would be an unexpected outcome from normal genetics, in which the colouring is usually the outcome of dominant or recessive gene alleles (see p. 99). The halfway colouring is due to what is called 'incomplete dominance'.

The search for the spotted cat

A breeding search is being carried out for the ultimate spotted cat; the quest arose from a belated recognition of the oldest natural breed of cats. The streets of Cairo are

Above A Tonkinese tests its reflexes on a toy mouse. The breed was invented in the sixties from a Siamese–Burmese cross, but its like already existed in south-east Asia as the ancient Copper cat.

Opposite The Egyptian Mau represents the oldest natural breed of cats; ironically, it was only recently recognised as a breed.

home to the most wonderful spotted tabbies with golden bronze bodies. Some are pets, while others follow the feral life. Princess Natalia Troubetskoye in Rome obtained a silver spotted female from Egypt, which she mated to a smoke spotted Egyptian tom from Rome; two bronze spotted kittens resulted, which she called Egyptian Maus. The Mau was recognised as a championship breed in North America only twenty-one years ago; this is ironic, for it can claim direct descent from the dawn of domestication in Ancient Egypt.

Above *Chocolate Oriental Spotted Tabbies were bred in an attempt to recreate the look of the cats of Ancient Egypt.*
Right *The California Spangled was created in the mid-eighties by an American cat breeder and writer, Paul Casey, and was launched by the department store Neiman Marcus in their Christmas catalogue. Casey developed the line to try to satisfy the public interest in spotted cats and lessen the pressures on wild species.*

Spot the ladies! Bengal cats and their owners. The breed is said to have acquired from its antecedents the best of both worlds: a wild cat's coat combined with a domestic cat's temperament.

The Oriental Spotted Tabby was a British attempt to recreate the look of the Ancient Egyptian cats from a Siamese-type tabby. In America, a Siamese crossed with an Abyssinian produced a kitten with ocelot-like spots – the first Ocicat.

Leopards for your living room

At Christmas 1986 a potential new breed, the California Spangled, gained notoriety when it was launched by the upmarket US department store Neiman Marcus. The store offered the new spotted cats as prestigious Christmas gifts, with a price tag of $1400 each. This way of promoting pets led to protest pickets from those who objected to animals being sold as status symbols.

The Bengal cat and other wild cat hybrids

A recent American creation, the Bengal cat, is nearer to the spotted wild cat pattern because it results from a cross between a true wild cat, the leopard cat (*Felis bengalensis*), and spotted ferals. At the 1991 TICA (The International Cat Association) Cat Show it was one of the most popular breeds – yet London Zoo had such a hybrid as far back as 1889. Remarkably, most wild cats will hybridise with the domestic cat; a British wild cat/domestic cat cross won first prize in the Spotted Tabby class at the 1873 Crystal Palace Show. Recently, further experimental hybrids have been bred, but unfortunately most are fairly aggressive. Bengal cat breeders, however, say they obtained the coat characteristics of the wild species while retaining the docile behaviour of the domestic cat.

A long, thin-bodied modern British Siamese with kittens. In the USA frailness of physique was so strongly bred for that the show breed collapsed.

10 Breeding for Breeding's Sake?

'*Again I must remind you that* . . . A CAT'S A CAT,' wrote T. S. Eliot in *Old Possum's Book of Practical Cats*. When is a cat not a cat? When you change it too much. Throughout history man has controlled dog breeding and selected mutations that were useful for a particular job of work; but when selection was made for showing purposes, genetic disasters occurred. In cat breeds, physical mutations that were previously allowed to perish are now being developed merely for the sake of difference. Not all are harmful, but some are achieved at considerable cost to the cat.

The crash of the American Siamese

The build of the Siamese has been taken to extremes. In North America until about 1980 it was the most popular shorthair show cat. Yet the unthinkable has happened, for at the main CFA and TICA shows in America in 1991 only a couple of cats were exhibited. What went wrong?

American and British breeders aimed to change the true Siamese into a more 'foreign' cat than the real thing, selecting for a longer-looking, thinner, lighter-built animal. Against historical authenticity, the US show schedules specified a 'dainty' cat. Frailer animals were

preferred, and long, tapering, wedge-shaped heads with flat foreheads. The point came when the show breed could be pushed no further and disastrously collapsed, for these genetically weak cats were prone to illness and breeding from them became difficult and uneconomic.

Viki Markstein of TICA and Richard Gebhardt, past President of the CFA, believe that, if the USA had followed the British example and embraced other colourpoint bred cats as Siamese, disaster could have been averted by having a wider genetic range. But would that have been enough? Lines were taken too far; there should be more regard for the authenticity of breed. The show bench cats need a genetic 'shot in the arm' from the natural breed in Thailand, or from robust pet lines of Siamese.

There is a remarkable difference between today's modern Peke-faced Persian (left) *and its nineteenth-century forebear with its more distinct and functional features* (above).

The Peke-faced Persian

Reduction of nose length has reached its peak, some American breeders claim, in the Peke-faced Persian. The British cat fancy considers it 'over-typed' – in other words, taken too far. The CFA standard states: 'Nose should be very short and depressed, or indented between the eyes. There should be a decidedly wrinkled muzzle.' It is hard to produce this shape without the animal suffering from breathing difficulties and faulty teeth. Even good type cats are prone to watering or running eyes as the draining ducts to the nose are compressed. This is breeding gone too far, yet it often wins top American honours.

The Scottish Fold and the American Curl

Giving a name to a genetic anomaly imparts apparent breed authenticity. In 1961, a Perthshire shepherd saw that the ears of a farmyard cat were folded forward flat on its head. From one kitten he started breeding a line.

The flattened ears give the cat a permanently sad expression. Matings are made to normal-eared cats, for if Fold cats are mated together any kittens which inherit the folded ear gene from both parents have an excess of cartilage around their joints, thickening of the tail and swelling feet.

The loss of one of the cat's key characteristics caused the GCCF to disallow registration, reasoning that the Fold might be prone to ear-mites and deafness. But no such fear inhibited the CFA, and by 1978 the breed was recognised with championship status. America became the centre for breeding, while Britain and Europe remain firm in considering the folded ears a deformity better not propagated.

Hot on its heels comes the American Curl. In 1981 a stray in California charmed her new owners with her unusual upward-curving ears. Preliminary acceptance by America's TICA and CFA was rapid.

A Scottish Fold mother and kitten. Unless Scottish Folds are mated with normal-eared cats, unpleasant abnormalities in the joints, tail and feet result.

The American Curl. Breeds such as this and the Scottish Fold are more readily accepted in the USA than in Britain.

THE BREEDS

The Manx cat

Of the two recognised cat breeds with truncated tails, genetically the Manx tail results from an incomplete dominant gene while that of the Japanese Bobtail comes from a recessive gene. Not all Manx are born in the 'rumpy' exhibition form; others show gradations of size of tail, classified as 'rumpy-risers', 'stumpies' and 'longies'. Despite folklore suggesting a hasty disembarkation from an Armada shipwreck the mutation probably occurred on the Isle of Man, where the cat's isolation would have enabled the gene to become established.

When the Manx tail gene is inherited from both parents it causes the kittens to die before birth: one in four conceptions from Manx–Manx matings do not develop.

The Rex cat – pitiable freak or desirable novelty? There are various kinds of Rex mutation, all producing a cat with a crimped-looking coat. This is a Devon Rex being judged.

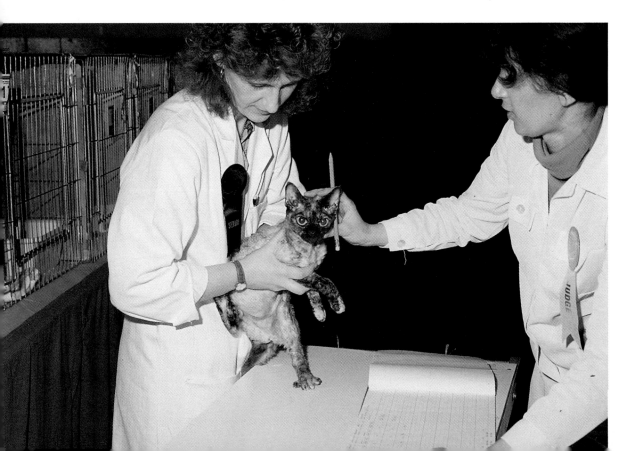

The Manx gene's effect often fuses vertebrae and the pelvis, and sometimes varying degrees of spina bifida are seen. Only the fact that the Manx is a historic breed stops us being as critical of this dangerous gene as of other more recent selected abnormalities.

The Rex cats

While to their admirers Rexes are distinctive cats with their unique short, crimped coat, to their detractors they are exactly that – cat wrecks! Rex cats were reported as freaks during the 1930s, but by the early 1950s changing attitudes saw novelty potential.

The first recognised Rex was born in 1950 in Cornwall; its trait was genetically recessive. A German Rex appeared in 1951, an American in Ohio in 1953 and in Oregon in 1959. Then in 1960 another English Rex appeared in Devon, close to the first. The two were initially thought to be the same, but when the Devon was mated with a Cornish Rex only normal-coated kittens were produced: despite their geographical proximity, each Rex parent was the result of a different gene. However German and Cornish Rexes were found to have the same genes, as they produced Rex kittens. So there are different genetic types.

Why does the Rex's coat look so different from that of other cats? A normal cat's coat has three main types of hair: the tall, coarse guard hairs, which stand above the coat; the awn hairs, which is what we see as 'coat'; and the down hairs of the underfur. The Devon Rex has all three, but severely distorted. In the Cornish, German and Oregon the guard hairs are absent. The Devon's hair is more fragile, and the follicle's bulb, in which each hair is embedded in the skin, smaller; as a result they commonly lick themselves bald. A near bald cat has a poor chance of survival in the wild, and even as pets Rexes are vulnerable to temperature changes.

In 1987 a new type of Rex mutation appeared in America. The Selkirk Rex is quite different on two counts: it has a dominant gene and a thick, curly, medium-length coat. For those who dislike other Rexes, its plush coat, solid build and distinctive curled whiskers may win them round.

The Sphynx

This animal is not the cat's whiskers – indeed it has no whiskers at all. If the Rex's degenerate coat worries some people, then the totally naked state of the Sphynx hairless cat is an abomination to most. Even Sphynx breeders have described the appearance of the cat as 'alien'. That some breeders decide to select such a disadvantaged animal deeply offends many people; but a hairless kitten

The hairless Sphynx would be quite unable to fend for itself and is therefore fully dependent on human beings.

born in 1966 in Ontario started a line recognised as a breed by a few North American societies.

The mutation may even have a reputable history from a hot climate, as an old Mexican hairless breed. A Mr and Mrs Shinick of Albuquerque, New Mexico, had a pair of hairless cats given to them in 1902 by the local Pueblo Indians. Jesuits living with the Indians said that these cats were the last of the Aztec breed.

The Munchkin

This startlingly stumpy-legged cat is the newest mutant to stumble on to the breed circuit in America. It is caused by the identical gene that gives a corgi or dachshund their short legs, according to geneticist Solveig Pflueger, and stems from two short-legged stray cats found in 1983. The mutation has occurred before, in the 1940s in Britain, and was described then in the *Veterinary Record* as 'having ferret-like movements, yet normal in other ways'.

The short legs of the Munchkin are caused by the same gene that makes dachshunds and corgis look as they do. Is this a view of the future for cats?

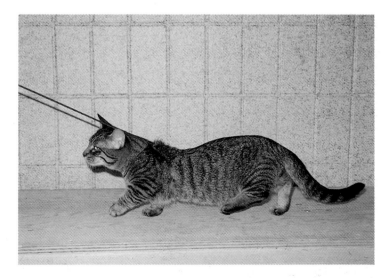

The present cat moves in the same way. Their line was first exhibited at TICA's 1991 Madison Square Garden Show; there was a lot of public interest, but caution was expressed by the cat fancy.

The day of the giant cat?

Much of the appeal of the enigmatic cat can be found in its natural grace and elegance, so the trend towards weirdness for its own sake is alarming – and at what cost to the cat? Someone, some time will present the world with a gross combination of a bald, flat-nosed, flat-eared, stumpy-legged, thin cat with no tail, on the terrible presumption that because it is possible it is all right. Suddenly it seems that the cat may be in danger of careering into the same range of shapes and sizes as the dog world, with all their associated genetic problems.

So far the cat's size is the one parameter that has not changed significantly, but it is surely just a matter of time before that comes about through mutation or genetic manipulative techniques. The concept of a domestic cat the size of a lion is unnerving, but the hybrids with wild species that have already been produced could be a step on the way. We accept Rottweilers as house pets despite their genetic selection for aggression, so who will challenge the inevitable insanity of large house cats wandering their neighbourhood?

The downside of breeding

Twenty-one years after founding the cat fancy Harrison Weir sadly wrote: 'I found the principal idea of many of its members consisted not so much in promoting the welfare of the cat as of winning prizes. I have left off judging of the cats, because I no longer cared to come into contact with such "Lovers of Cats".'

Has Harrison Weir's well-intended plan for the rehabilitation of cats turned sour? Breeders have produced some superb cats, but the system of judging means that extremes are sometimes sought. For the cat, health and genetic problems may be the outcome.

Fortunately even in the USA the moggie – or mutt, as it is known there – is still the commonest cat, but the growing percentage of breed cats will increase the proportion of the population that suffers from genetic problems. Geneticist Roy Robinson notes that when breeds become extremely popular 'the temptation is to breed from every animal, even from those which would normally be discarded'. Showing produces undeniably wonderful cats, but the very system of a rigorous application of schedule points pushes breeding to extremes. When the basis on which some new breeds are given their status consists of

serious defects, pause for thought is needed before the world of domestic cats becomes full of genetic problems.

Although responsible members of the cat fancy try to prevent excesses, selecting for breeds inevitably creates problems. Inbreeding is essential if a particular breed conformation is to be sustained, but the resulting animals obviously lack the relative genetic randomness exercised by the moggie, and therefore also its vigour.

Show judges should not go for extremes. If the breed standard specifies a short nose, it should be shorter than that of other breeds – it should not be a question of the shortest nose winning. As Richard Gebhardt, long-time President and Chairman of the Cat Fanciers' Association, put it: 'For many years the CFA had taken the position that a breed was determined by what it was bred from and not how it looked. Today more careful study and the growing interest in, and understanding of, genetics has altered some of the earlier thinking.'

The continued existence of old breeds in their places of origin – the Egyptian cat, the Angora and the Siamese – proves that breeds can survive if given a certain genetic freedom. It is ironic that most breeders would be more sure of the authenticity of an Egyptian Mau with championship and pedigree papers in America than of the real thing on the streets of Cairo. The very process of selection to a standard takes the show breed away from the natural breed.

Why do some breeders want to produce extreme forms, even to the perpetual discomfort of the animals? There is a strong attraction in the flat face and large eyes of the Persian, for it is a perpetuation of the endearing kitten face. The great Victorian/Edwardian cat illustrator Louis Wain made his career from drawing the large eyes and flat faces of Persian kittens. He owed his popularity to

The artist Louis Wain (1860–1939) was famous for his anthropomorphic portrayals of kitten-faced cats which satisfied owners' psychological need for surrogate children who would never grow up. This painting is entitled The Cats' Tea Party.

portraying many owners' sentiments towards their surrogate children, who, like Peter Pan, never grew up.

It is an extension of the changes that occurred during domestication, when juvenile characteristics in behaviour were sought. But how far should we go? Not long ago a breed appeared in California that seemed to be the utter denigration of the spirit of the cat. The Rag Doll, which gained its name from its habit of going limp when picked up, was claimed to be the ultimate docile cat. Here was a living soft toy for skyscraper apartments – a cushion cat, a designer accessory. The Sphynx has built-in dependency, as it needs constant warmth. The modern show Persian must be combed daily or its fur becomes seriously knotted. The centuries-old independent identity of the cat is being sacrificed in favour of making dependent toys, unable to survive without protection and constant attention.

Natural breeding selected for function, giving a healthy, good-looking cat. Now, in the brief span under our control, are we in danger of ruining it? When an animal with such natural perfection of design is changed, then most changes are not going to be improvements, particularly when weirdness is the criterion for choice. A conformation causing physical disadvantage should be challenged if it were proposed for a breed. The show bench has given us some marvellous cats, like the Somali and the Balinese, but so has natural breeding with slight artificial selection around the world.

Moggies have always looked after their own breeding, but fewer can do so today since up to 90 per cent of house cats are neutered. Feral cats often breed with house cats, but for the last decade neutering of feral colonies has been pursued by various organisations in Britain and the USA. Since breed cats are therefore set to become an ever larger part of the cat population, will the traditional robustness of the moggie still ensure the salvation of the cat?

Is this the ultimate dependent cat? The Rag Doll, seen here with its Californian inventor, goes limp when picked up.

Man and Cat

A perfect partnership: warmth and comfort for the cat, reduction of stress for the owner.

*Cat welfare at the turn of the
century: the cart of the Royal
London Institution for
Lost and Starving Cats,
about 1903.*

11 What Price Dependency?

The human/cat world has three distinct and separate sub-cultures: show cat breeders, feral cat colony feeders and trappers, and the average house cat owner. One common motivation is the establishment of dependency in the cat.

Cat welfare

Animal welfare may seem a largely modern phenomenon. However Britain's Cats' Protection League is over sixty years old, and at the turn of the century there were several cat refuges in London.

One alternative to putting down a stray is New Jersey's Associated Humane Societies' scheme. You adopt one chosen from a videotape, and pay to support it at Animal Haven Farm.

For feral groups there are other ways. Whenever a colony is destroyed, the resulting vacuum fills with other cats; but neutering the cats and then returning them to their site avoids this and checks the population. A holiday in Venice led to twenty-five years' dedication to the welfare of the street cats of the city by Englishwoman Helena Sanders. Feral cats have been reduced to a more manageable population largely due to DINGO, an Anglo-

Venetian cat charity started by Mrs Sanders and her friends.

'Saving' feral cats used to large ranges by incarcerating them in a small pen is not kind. From cardboard boxes in London to the wooden cat 'condos' of San Francisco, temporary lodges for independent cats sprout, provided by those who feel the cat is only a lap animal and can't survive without their help.

Cat company

In the UK there are now nearly 7 million cats, and in the USA 51–57 million according to petfood manufacturers. Throughout the 1980s the owned cat population in both countries went up by a staggering 30 per cent. Why?

In the south-east of England more young yuppie owner-occupiers of the AB socio-economic group have cats than any other pet. People in apartments, with less space and less time to walk the dog, can still cuddle the cat; and people who are out all day often have a second cat as company for the first: 35 per cent of British and 42 per cent of American cat-owning households now have two.

But why have pets at all? For many people, including the modern yuppie, they can play the role of an undemanding, perpetual child that is simple to care for. Young professional couples nowadays often delay having children, and the cat in particular acts as a substitute. Companionship heads the list of reasons why owners say they want a cat. With today's work pressures, marriages breaking up and people living alone, there is great need for a companion who will give quiet reassurance. The cat is a therapist's dream!

Pet owners seem to live longer than non-pet owners. Stroking a cat lessens stress and reduces blood pressure.

Above *In Boca Raton, Florida, human intervention ensures that abandoned or unwanted cats receive care and attention.*

Studies of people who have brought cats into their lives have shown that after a year the new owners felt less anxious, lonely or depressed. Institutionalised elderly people and other patients generally benefit because it enables them to socialise more.

How good are we for cats?

Left *Older people and cats often provide mutual companionship.*

An American study found that a third of all pet cats were overweight, blaming the pet food industry for putting too much effort into making food palatable so as to obtain a larger market. Owners like to buy food that their cats vacuum up and often give them more than is ideal.

American cats consume over $2.75 billion worth a year of commercial cat food, while British cats eat £480 million worth. The implication is that in Britain we pay £70 a year for a cat's food, yet America seems to spend just $50, a third of that spent on the British moggie. Perhaps Americans buy more fresh food or serve left-overs.

Caught food like mice is balanced, but the human diet does not suit the cat. The minimum protein requirement of an adult cat is four times that of either the dog or us, and without certain amino acids the cat becomes ill: if there is insufficient argenine in the diet severe ammonia toxicity develops, and lack of taurine results in blindness. The preparation of a suitable balance is so complex that it is safer to use nutritionally complete commercial foods.

The in-house cat

In the USA the house cat has become the house-bound cat. During the 1980s the majority of the American *Cat Fancy* magazine's readers' cats changed from an indoor/outdoor to a strictly indoor existence. This arose from their owners' paranoia about the risk of disease from other cats, and fear of traffic accidents. In urban New York these worries are understandable, but in the wilds cats are jailed for the same reasons.

A house-bound cat shreds furniture, and so, forced by public pressure, declawing of the front paws is common veterinary practice in the USA – to the horror of British vets. It is not a stronger sort of nail-clipping, but amputation under general anaesthetic. American vets face the unhappy choice of declawing an animal or killing it. To render a cat defenceless and unable to climb is to sentence it to house-bound internment, and to destroy something of the essential cat.

Unsurprisingly, the inventor of cat litter was an American, Ed Lowe, who forty years ago suggested using absorbent clay in his neighbour's cat's earth-box. He started a business that now has sales of over £300 million a year. A real measure of the changed lifestyle of American cats is that an incredible 70 per cent of owners buy cat litter, and a large part of this figure relates to rural cats. In Britain, where cats can go outside, the comparable figure is 15–20 per cent.

Behaviour problems

In America the commonest behavioural problem with captive cats is fouling. The trapped cat may not like the texture or the smell of the litter and find something it prefers – like your carpet. In a Pennsylvanian study virtually all owners viewed their cat as a family member, so for the majority its behavioural 'problems' are not a reason to get rid of it. Most 'problems' concern behaviour that people don't want in their house. Cats allowed outside are less likely to foul your home and rip the furniture.

Cat shrinks

Who needs help when things go wrong in the cat-human relationship? Dr Peter Borchelt, a cat psychologist working in a New York veterinary hospital, denies it is just neurotic people who need treating rather than the cats. Often owners unknowingly make inappropriate signals to the cat.

In America, inevitably, problems occur as a result of imprisonment, and cats seen as wilfully destructive or aggressive are often declawed as a first resort. Peter provides an alternative. An 'aggressive' cat may just be

exerting its playfulness and predatory instincts. As part of the cat's group we must expect some play directed at us, including ritualised catching and fighting.

Among the apartment-imprisoned cats in the USA behaviour 'problems' inevitably arise. In New York the high-rise cat owner can be helped by cat psychologist Peter Borchelt.

Changing worlds

Many people just like cats, but various factors colour this relationship. We consider them 'family members' and child substitutes, and make them captive, dependent toys. Neutering keeps them in the non-sexual juvenile world.

THE RAYBURN NOUVELLE

The heart of the home, providing food, warmth and comfort – what better symbol could Rayburn have chosen for their product than a cat? (Adapted from a Rayburn advertising brochure.)

Despite all this the sexual image does not fade. In commercials for jewellery or coffee, elegant cat languishes alongside elegant woman. The cat can also be a reassuring symbol of hearth and home - cat alongside mother. It still has the dual role of the fertility goddess Bastet.

For three and a half thousand years the cat remained beside us but retained its independence. Now we run the risk of ruining the ultimate free spirit - the cat. But unexpectedly, in death we turn full circle and mimic the ancient world.

Cat cemeteries and the American way of death

Cemeteries for cats are far more common in the USA than in Britain and Europe, for in many American cities it is illegal to bury pets in your own backyard, and in any case a large proportion of cat owners live in towns and have no gardens. From Pet Rest Inc., Ohio, comes the Pet Rest Burial Receptacle, a water- and airtight cat coffin with 'personalised name identification' and a 'sample memorial service'. If this seems symptomatic of our rampant consumer society, remember the extensive cat necropolises of Ancient Egypt. What for some seems a charade brings comfort to others, who may feel as much grief over the loss of a beloved pet as they would for a relative.

Florida offers freeze-drying for a mere $1000 in the ultimate attempt to keep your pet – to pretend, like the Ancient Egyptians, that you have cheated death. Are these the modern mummies that future generations will look back to and say, 'Ah, that was a cat!'?

Opposite *Further echoes of ancient Bubastis – a cat restorer in Los Angeles adds the finishing touches to a freeze-dried loved one.*

Above *Hygiene regulations make pet cemeteries part of American society: but is a gravestone in Florida so far removed in spirit from a sarcophagus in Thebes?*

Further Reading

This list contains both titles of a general nature and more academic works for those who wish to read in detail about particular topics mentioned in this book.

Armitage, P. L. and Clutton-Brock, Juliet, 'A Radiological and Historical Investigation into the Mummification of Cats from Ancient Egypt', *Journal of Archaeological Science*, 8: 185-196 (1981).

Baines, John and Malek, Jaromir, *Atlas of Ancient Egypt* (Phaidon Press Ltd, 1980).

Baldwin, James A., 'Ships and the early diffusion of the domestic cat', *Carnivore Genetics Newsletter*, 4: 32-33 (1979).

Borchelt, Peter I. and Voith, Victoria L., 'Aggressive Behavior in Dogs and Cats', *The Compendium on Continuing Education*, Vol. 7, No. 11, November 1985.

Clutton-Brock, Juliet, *The British Museum Book of Cats* (British Museum Publications, 1988).

Conway, William Martin, *Dawn of Art in the Ancient World* (Percival and Co., 1891).

Gebhardt, Richard, *A Standard Guide to Cat Breeds* (Trewin Copplestone/Macmillan, 1979)

Hornidge, Marilis, *That Yankee Cat* (The Harpswell Press, 1981).

Howey, M. Oldfield, *The Cat in the Mysteries of Religion and Magic* (Rider and Co., 1930). Reprinted as *The Cat in Magic, Mythology, and Religion* (Bracken Books, 1989).

Macfarlane, A. D. J., *Witchcraft Prosecutions in Essex 1560-1680* (D. Phil. thesis, Oxford University, 1967).

Martin, Edward J., *The Trial of the Templars* (George Allen and Unwin Ltd, 1928).

Morrison-Scott, T., 'The Mummified Cats of Ancient Egypt', *Proceedings of the Zoological Society of London*, 21: 861-867 (1952).

Naville, Edouard, 'Bubastis 1887-1889', 8th Memoir of the Egypt Exploration Fund (Kegan Paul Trench, 1891).

Necker, Claire, *The Natural History of Cats* (A. S. Barnes & Co. Inc., 1970).

Petrie, Flinders, *Tombs of the Courtiers and Oxyrhynkhos* (British School of Archaeology in Egypt, 1925).

Robinson, Roy, *Genetics for Cat Breeders* (Pergamon Press, 1977).

Searle, A. G., 'A Study of Variation in Singapore Cats', *Journal of Genetics*, 56: 111-127 (1959).

Simpson, Frances, *The Book of the Cat* (Cassell & Co., 1903).

Stahl, Philippe, *Le Chat Forestier d'Europe (Felis silvestris): Exploitation des Ressources et Organisation Spatiale* (Centre National d'études sur la rage et la pathologie des animaux sauvages, 1986).

Tabor, Roger, 'The Changing Life of Feral Cats At Home And Abroad', *Zoological Journal of the Linnean Society* 95: 151-161 (1989).

Tabor, Roger, 'Origins of Essex Cats', *The Essex Field Club Bulletin*, 29 (1984).

Tabor, Roger, *The Wild Life of the Domestic Cat* (Arrow Books, 1983).

Todd, Neil, 'Cats and Commerce', *Scientific American*, 237: 100-107 (1977).

Turner, Dennis C. and Bateson, Patrick, *The Domestic Cat* (Cambridge University Press, 1988).

Weir, Harrison, *Our Cats and All about Them* (R. Clements and Co., 1889).

Wilson, Edward, *Diary of the 'Terra Nova' Expedition to the Antarctic 1910-1912* (Blandford Press, 1972).

Wilson, Meredith, *Encyclopedia of American Cat Breeds* (T. F. H. Publications, Inc., 1978)

Wright, Michael and Walters, Sally (eds) *The Book of the Cat* (Pan Books, 1980).

Zeuner, F. E., *A History of Domesticated Animals* (Hutchinson, 1963).

Index

Index